BLIND FAITH

BLIND FAITH

Seeing God Through Darkness

CHAD ROBERTS

979-8-3845-2860-9

Published by B&H Publishing Group
Brentwood, Tennessee

Published in association with Yates & Yates, LLP.
www.yates2.com.

Dewey Decimal Classification: 234.2
Subject Heading: FAITH / SUFFERING / JOY AND SORROW

Cover design by Faceout Studio. Author photo by Brad Lovell.

1 2 3 4 5 • 29 28 27 26

To my beautiful wife, Sadie.

This book is affectionately dedicated to you, because you are the inspiration in all that I do. Nine years into our marriage, our world went unexpectedly dark, yet you remain the brightest light for me, Piper, Emmy, Hudson, and John Mark. Together we navigate storms and celebrate triumphs.

I love you!

Acknowledgments

I want to thank my remarkable executive assistant, Michole Wampler. Together we have learned and navigated the complexities of writing and publishing. This book would have never happened without your tireless efforts and attention to details. It is as much yours as it is mine. You make my thoughts become visible. You are more than a coworker. You are a great friend to me and my family.

My heartfelt gratitude to my executive staff. When I first went blind, a world of pressure fell on you. Your leadership has been invaluable, as you have navigated our church through many challenges and led us to great victories. I love serving alongside you. Through our shared vision and purpose, we are laboring together to build His church.

I would like to thank my incredible congregation, Preaching Christ Church. The greatest honor of my life is being your shepherd. My chief responsibility is to shepherd the flock (1 Pet. 5:2). Every sermon I preach and the spiritual content I create is first and foremost for you. Thank you for loving God's Kingdom more than our little building and our little community. You are a local church with a global reach.

I am so grateful to my literary agents, Sealy Yates and Matt Yates. Your expertise has coached me toward my lifelong dream.

You believed in me when, at times, I did not believe in myself. Thank you for giving me opportunities and opening extraordinary doors. I cannot express how proud I feel to be an author with Yates & Yates.

I want to thank the amazing team at Lifeway and B&H Publishing. You have made the journey of being a first-time author an exhilarating one. A heartfelt thanks to Mary Wiley for believing in me and helping bring the message of this book to the world. Your insights, advice, and constant encouragement carried me across the finish line. An additional thanks to Matthew Jordan for the superb editing, as well as the entire Lifeway team who have worked behind the scenes to make this project a reality.

Last, I want to thank the numerous friends, supporters, and leaders who have blessed my life. I especially thank Robert J. Morgan, Terry Whitson, Joy Bollinger, and Joe Herron. You have been friends, mentors, and trusted confidants.

Contents

A Word to the Reader

Dear Reader,

Thank you for reading this book. I know your time is valuable. It is my hope that the truths within these pages will strengthen and deepen your faith. It is more than a collection of words. It is a journey of Scriptures, lessons, and experiences God has taught me through my own season of suffering. If the message of this book encourages you, consider sharing it with others. I would love to hear your thoughts and know how to pray for you. You can email me directly at pastorchadroberts@gmail.com or visit my website, chadroberts.org.

Happy reading,

Pastor Chad

Introduction

Light in the Darkness

When I pictured my life, I never imagined blindness. Yet at age thirty-eight, it became my reality. As a pastor and a lifelong Christ-follower, I was asking the same question that many ask: "If God is good, then why am I going through this?"

What would be the beginning of my blindness began on a mission trip in Central America where I was invited to train pastors. A group of us decided to hike a large mountain to visit a Christian radio tower. When I reached the top, I felt blood vessels burst behind my left eye. It was like looking through a spiderweb of blood. You can imagine the fear and questions that flooded my mind. *What did I do to deserve this? How could God allow it? Why did He not prevent it?*

While blindness may be unique to me, suffering is common to us all. At some point, everyone experiences loss. Perhaps you are in a place in life where you find yourself with more questions than answers. If so, this book is for you. Far more than my personal narrative, this book is about God's faithfulness through difficult seasons. We often feel frustrated when we cannot make sense of God's plan or see His purpose in our pain. The chapters that follow will help you recognize God's goodness even when the outcomes of life do not appear good.

As my eyesight rapidly deteriorated into complete blindness, rather than resigning to a life of disability, I began to gain a contentment that only comes by waiting on God. I chose to move forward and not remain stuck in suffering. And yes, there have been days when I could not smile, so I learned to laugh. There have been days that I did not want to get out of bed, so I learned to say, "This is the day the LORD has made; [I will] rejoice and be glad in it" (Ps. 118:24 CSB).

I found a well that has quenched my thirsting, and I simply want to guide you to that same well of grace as you walk your own road of suffering, seeking to recognize God's constant hand of goodness.

The Gathering Storm

I sat in an oversized brown-leather exam chair when the doctor came back into the room. I didn't like the look on his face. He sat across from me and said, "Tell me again what happened with your vision when you were out of the country." I had already told him the story once, but after examining my eyes, it was clear he wanted more details. I took a deep breath, pursed my lips, and told him my story from the beginning. The doctor responded, "Before I decide on surgery, let me run one more test." After running the last test and looking at the results, the doctor said bluntly, "Chad, you have a storm brewing in your eyes. You have no choice but to undergo surgery. Don't worry about anything.

I've done more of these than I can count, and you are in good hands." Before leaving the room, he joked and said, "Whatever you do, don't google pictures of the procedure." I had never faced a surgery, so the thought of someone operating on my eyes instantly made me feel uneasy and queasy.

The first surgery required putting a gas bubble behind my eye, which then necessitated two weeks of bed rest while the eye healed. Unfortunately, the surgery was not successful. Immediately after the two weeks of recovery, I faced a second surgery on the same eye. This time, they removed the gas bubble and put in a type of silicone. Tragically, the surgeon made a horrific mistake and tore my retina, leaving me permanently blind in my left eye.

Fifteen months after this surgery, I lost complete vision in both eyes. As I thought about it, I realized I had never even had a real conversation with a blind person. I prepared the best I could mentally, emotionally, and, most of all, spiritually. It seemed the pressures of life were converging all at once. When blindness finally arrived, my daughters, Piper and Emmy, were eight and six years old. My son, Hudson, was born the spring that I had the failed surgeries, and our youngest son, John Mark, was born only three months before I lost complete vision. You can imagine the strain and pressures blindness put on my wife, Sadie, and our growing family.

During this time, the national office retail chain, Staples, ran humorous commercials that featured a large red button called "The Easy Button." One night, while lying in bed, I distinctly remember feeling the weight of all these pressures. Tears filled my eyes as I asked the Lord if I could just hit a heavenly easy button. The Lord took me to Acts 14:22: "Strengthening the souls of the disciples, encouraging them to continue in the faith, and saying that through many tribulations we must enter the kingdom of God."

It is one thing to speak, write, and counsel about suffering. It is another thing to walk through it personally. You will learn through the pages of this book how to not despise your sufferings. Paul was able to say to the Philippian church: "Brothers, . . . what has happened to me has really served to advance the gospel" (Phil. 1:12). This means the hardships of our lives are not pointless nor meaningless. Rather, they serve to advance the gospel. Is that how you see life's hurts and disappointments?

Christ's invitation is this: "Come to me, all who labor and are heavy laden, and I will give you rest. Take my yoke upon you, and learn from me, for I am gentle and lowly in heart, and you will find rest for your souls. For my yoke is easy, and my burden is light" (Matt. 11:28–30). As my eyesight diminished, I began to understand what it is to take on a yoke, and I have found the yoke of blindness exactly as Jesus described it—light, easy, and well-fitted.

In a final attempt to save my vision, I was sent to Duke University. I was eager to receive world-class care from the most elite eye doctors available. Just as the Lord had prepared me for every step through this valley, there was more He was about to teach me. With each passing week, my vision decreased, but my resolve deepened from Sunday to Sunday.

If you knew you were going blind, how would you react and how would you prepare? When people ask me what it is like to go from a fully sighted person to a blind man, my answer is always the same . . . surprising. I am surprised at how much closer this experience has brought me to my wife and children. I am a better husband and better father blind than I was with sight. I am more present in the room and more attentive than ever before. I am surprised that I do not miss social media, movies, and other distractions. I thought not being able to use my phone, tablet, and laptop would be awful. Turns out, I do not miss them at all. Mostly and above all, I am surprised at God's grace. He has caused all grace to abound toward me with every twist and turn along this road.

Part of that grace is a sense of humor. I like to tell my church family that I am like a Roomba vacuum cleaner. When I run into things, I rescan and go a different direction. I tell them that the only things that scare me are high curbs and half-open doors! One of the first Sundays I preached blind, I could feel the tension in the church as people wondered if I could continue to preach and pastor completely blind. I decided to play a prank. When I got to the pulpit, I turned my back to the congregation and welcomed everyone that Sunday. I heard a collective gasp from the listeners as they thought I was blind and confused. I turned around laughing, telling them I was only joking. It felt like the ice broke that day, and we have never looked back since.

A Front-Row Seat to God's Miracles

People will sometimes ask me if I am angry with God for allowing blindness to come in the prime of life. Paul described his physical affliction as "a thorn was given me in the flesh" (2 Cor. 12:7). Shortly after going blind, I had to transition my vast library of books into audio titles. One of the first audiobooks I enjoyed was *An Unhurried Life* by Alan Fadling. He observes that Paul uses the word *given* when describing the thorn in his flesh. I determined then that I was not going to view blindness as a setback, but as a gift from the Lord to be used in a most special way.

I knew I could make this resolve because of God's promise in 2 Corinthians 12:9, "My grace is sufficient for you, for my power is made perfect in weakness." As I transitioned into quite literally the darkest season of my life, I knew with a head knowledge that God's grace would be sufficient. Now, I needed to know it with my whole heart.

I had seen God move, and in so many ways, God had allowed me to live ten lifetimes leading up to the point of blindness. At just twelve years old, I had a great hunger for the Lord and people sensed a call of God on my life, so much so that God provided an opportunity to serve internationally across an entire summer with a family friend who left a comfortable life in Tennessee to serve in Romania. My parents struggled with allowing me to go because of my age, so they told me I'd need to raise all of my own funds, hoping that would derail the trip. Yet, God provided again and again as people handed me envelopes, explaining that the Lord had asked them to give money to me for this trip. To my parents' amazement, we watched God supply over and over until the trip was completely paid for. More than the financial provision, it was the Lord who clearly spoke to my parents' hearts, assuring them that if they released me into His hands, He would protect me, and He did across the following summers as I traveled through Germany, Hungary, Romania, and Ukraine.

These experiences and the insatiable desire for God to be glorified in my life and among those I might have the opportunity to serve set my course. I was serious about serving God, but I was stunned when I felt God directing me to plant a church at age twenty. I gave excuses: "I'm far too young. I'm not married. I don't have children. Families will not come where there is a single pastor." Despite my arguments, I could not persuade Him. I knew in my heart that if I did not step out in faith and plant this church from scratch, that I would be living in willful, sinful disobedience. So, with ten people, Preaching Christ Church was formed in 2001. During those years of trying to gain traction, I would remind the Lord that I was right about people believing I was too young to pastor, and again, God was proven to be faithful. He brought families to call this church home and moved among us, despite my doubts.

Throughout my life and ministry, I have had a front-row seat to God's miracles. So, when blindness suddenly entered my life in 2018, I looked back at God's track record. From my youth, God had been completely reliable. The same faith it took to go on mission trips as a kid and the same faith it took to plant a church was the same faith it would take to face the life-altering handicap of blindness. If God's grace had sustained me through the various seasons of my life, would His grace not be sufficient now? As darkness closed in on me, my resolve deepened. I would move forward in God's plan no matter what I faced along the way.

One of my favorite hymns is "Turn Your Eyes Upon Jesus," written in 1922 by Helen Lemmel, who also suffered from late-onset blindness. Now that I am well along the path of blindness, I find the lyrics of this song inspiring.

"Turn Your Eyes Upon Jesus"

by Helen Lemmel

O soul, are you weary and troubled?
No light in the darkness you see?
There's light for a look at the Savior,
And life more abundant and free!

Turn your eyes upon Jesus,
Look full in His wonderful face,
And the things of earth will grow strangely dim,
In the light of His glory and grace.[1]

I don't need working physical eyes to seek the face of Jesus, no matter what suffering may come. To turn our eyes from our own situations to the eternal truth of what God has done for us in Christ will cause our sufferings to "grow strangely dim," not that they don't matter and not that they don't hurt, but that the glory of God is so much better. He is better.

Chapter 1

Seeing God in the Deep Shadows

In the classic devotional book *Streams in the Desert*, the story is told of a nineteenth-century lacemaker:

> In the famous lace shops of Brussels, there are certain rooms devoted to the spinning of the finest and most delicate patterns. These rooms are altogether darkened, save for a light from one very small window, which falls directly upon the pattern. There is only one spinner in the room, and he sits where the narrow stream of light falls upon the threads of his weaving. "Thus," we are told by the guide, "do we secure our choicest products. Lace is always more delicately and beautifully woven when the worker himself is in the dark and only his pattern is in the light."[2]

Sometimes we also find ourselves in the dark with what seems like only a small light to see the good pattern God is weaving for our lives, struggling to make sense of it all or finding the beauty or good in our experience. Yet if we are faithful and persevere, the day will come when we realize that "the most exquisite work" was done in those days of darkness. "If you are in the deep shadows because of some strange, mysterious providence, do not be afraid. Simply go on in faith and love, never doubting. God is watching, and He will bring good and beauty out of all your pain and tears."[3]

We see this promise in Isaiah 45:3 (NLT): "And I will give you treasures hidden in the darkness—secret riches. I will do this so you may know that I am the LORD, the God of Israel, the one who calls you by name." The darkness I live with has yielded great treasures. God has taught me my greatest lessons through my deepest suffering, and the lessons have not been wasted.

It has been well said that what is painful in life can become profitable. Have you ever seen a caterpillar struggling in a cocoon? If an ugly, earthbound caterpillar wants to transform into a heavenly butterfly, it must go through a cocoon experience. In Romans 12:2, Paul wrote that we are to be "transformed." The Greek word for "transformed," *metamorphoō*, is where we get our English word *metamorphosis*. This type of change is only accomplished through a transformational process. In the case of a caterpillar, it is a painful process to be transformed into a butterfly. So it is for us spiritually. God does His best work in a process, and if we are going to become "conformed to the image of his Son" (Rom. 8:29), then we must be willing to go through the painful process. God's cocoon is a place of preparation. We store up hope for today so that we may face the pain of transformation tomorrow as that comes through molding and shaping, suffering and conviction.

Months before I knew that eye surgery would be needed, I began preaching through the book of Acts. A few weeks into the series, I felt compelled by the Holy Spirit to preach without notes. This confused me because I had a special fondness for my sermon notes. However, I listened and obeyed, and from that Sunday on I prepared like I always did, except I did not take notes to the pulpit. Little did I know that God was preparing me even then to preach in total blindness.

Today, I preach without a Bible or any notes, because God has replaced those notes with an ability to memorize Scripture line upon line. Sometimes I think how good it feels to leave my house on Sunday mornings, completely equipped and empowered by the Holy Spirit to feed God's sheep without the aid of notes or a physical Bible. Walking out this process has truly taught me how to hide God's Word in my heart (Ps. 119:11).

Are you experiencing God's cocoon and struggling to understand why life is challenging? It could be that God is wanting to transform you. Perhaps your marriage, a job loss, a health crisis, or some other interruption in the rhythm of your life is bringing about struggle and questioning. But take heart because you are most likely in God's process of transformation and what is painful will ultimately be profitable. This profit may not look like earthly treasure. It may not seem to be profitable on this side of heaven in the world's opinion, but it will transform you so that you look more and more like Jesus. God will not abandon you in the middle of the process as He works in you. The question is: Will you yield to God and to the process?

Our Limited Vision

It is easier to submit to God's plans when we understand the purpose behind them. When we see that God is not random nor coincidental but is intentional in what He allows in our lives, then we begin to gain His perspective rather than our own limited view. Our limitations are much like Norman Rockwell's 1958 painting *Knothole Baseball*, which portrays a limited view of a baseball game through the knothole of a fence. Much the same, without the help of Scripture, our understanding of God is as limited as viewing a baseball game through a knothole.

When we consider our present sufferings, our understanding may seem limited. What a believer must do is simply look back at the faithfulness of God. When we realize God's track record and reliability, it will strengthen our faith for the present and the future. Although we may not be able to see far into tomorrow, Scripture reassures us that we can see our next few steps. "Your word is a lamp to my feet and a light to my path" (Ps. 119:105). This is what it means to walk by faith.

The perspective we should seek to gain in suffering should not be our own, but God's perspective. I often find that God sees life differently than I do. Rather than exhausting my energy, trying to make sense of my sufferings, I should rest and trust that God has purpose in all that He allows. The reality is many of us will never understand the reason God permits our hurts this side of heaven. Corrie ten Boom, a survivor of a Nazi concentration camp, once observed the experiences of this life like that of a tapestry. The front side is a beautiful piece of art, yet the back side is ugly and chaotic. You cannot tell from the back side what the artist has in mind until you flip the tapestry over. So it is in this life. When you pray and look up to God, remember that you are looking at the bottom of the tapestry. You will not be able to see His full plan until heaven. This is why you can still trust in His goodness and faithfulness. There is a reason to your pain.

Gaining Through Losing

My wife, Sadie, and I often tell people that it took losing eyesight to gain the greatest treasures that we are experiencing today. David wrote: "He makes me to lie down in green pastures" (Ps. 23:2 NKJV). And that is what God did for me after losing sight. When sighted, I did everything fast. I worked fast, talked fast, and drove fast. I am embarrassed to admit how many times I was pulled over for speeding. So, you can imagine what the weeks and months were like when blindness brought my life to a grinding halt and God was making me lie down in green pastures.

My life as I knew it no longer existed. There was no more zipping through town and rushing from meeting to meeting. Instead, I was standing in my driveway with my backpack, waiting for someone to pick me up to take me to work. I felt like a kid waiting for a ride to school. It was a painful and humbling struggle to slow down and let others help me. Yet the Lord showed me that it was His hand making me "to lie down in green pastures." It was in those lush "green pastures" that my soul found a peace that I had never known. I began to walk in a sweet contentment I never knew existed.

We often hear Philippians 4:13 (NKJV): "I can do all things through Christ who strengthens me." But what does this verse really mean? Paul explains: "Not that I am speaking of being in need, for I have learned, in whatever situation I am, to be content. I know how to be brought low, and I know how to abound. In any and every circumstance, I have learned the secret of facing plenty and hunger, abundance and need" (Phil. 4:11–12). Paul taught that the secret to contentment does not lie in our circumstances, whether pleasant or uncomfortable. Rather, contentment rises above all circumstances because it is a choice.

Despite the situation that we may be in, we must determine if we are willing to embrace contentment. As we allow the Lord to make us lie down in green pastures, we discover what it means to "be still, and know that I am God" (Ps. 46:10). Contentment is found in stillness. I am not interested in the rat race of life. Busyness only robs us from experiencing the joy of contentment. Instead, I want the lush green pastures God has for me.

Three months into blindness, I went on a retreat in the mountains with all the small group leaders from my church. I was adjusting the best I could, but the last place I wanted to be was outside of my comfort zone. On Saturday morning, most of the group was going on a hike. I felt that the mountainous area might be a little too dangerous for a new blind guy. So, I told Sadie I would stay behind in the cabin and listen to something on my phone. The internet had worked well the night before, but to my shock, I had no internet service after everyone had left. I remember feeling so frustrated. There was nothing to do. Once again, I found myself in God's cocoon, alone with just my thoughts and the Lord.

Frustration began to diminish as I began to pray. Rather than telling God how He could make my life better and easier, I began to call on the name of the Lord and seek contentment in Him. What I thought was going to be a frustrating day alone with nothing to do turned into one of the sweetest times I have ever spent with the Lord. That day is when I began appreciating God's green pastures and the contentment God could teach me there.

Self-Control: The Right Response

As I continued to learn contentment, the Lord taught me that there was more work He wanted to do in me—namely, developing self-control. It can feel overwhelming when we consider all the areas of life that are beyond our power. We cannot control the actions of other people. We are unable to control certain things our bodies do, such as the bursting of blood vessels behind the eyes. Very little is within our control. However, what I have learned is the one thing I can control is my response. I may not be able to help what happens to me, but I can certainly decide how to respond to it.

It is interesting what Paul wrote to the believers in Philippi when he said, "Let your reasonableness be known to everyone.

The Lord is at hand" (Phil. 4:5). The word *reasonableness* literally means a right reaction or, you could say, a mature response. It is the opposite of someone who overreacts. Think how much pain we could avoid if we did not overreact. How many of us can relate to this?

Prior to blindness, I did not pay much attention to my dreams. Now, I love to dream because I see everything in vivid color. When my kids ask me what it is like to be blind, I laugh and say, "Well, I'm only blind half the time. The other half, I am dreaming." However, in the beginning of my journey with blindness, dreams were difficult for me. I can't fully express what it was like to wake up from a vivid dream and see nothing but darkness. Those days I did not want to get out of bed. My overreaction would fuel despair and depression that caused me to be withdrawn and reclusive. Other days, I was joyful and productive. The problem was that I never knew what kind of day I would have. I felt at the mercy of my emotions. This is where the Lord began to teach me self-control.

We are like a pendulum that often swings wildly. Either we swing one way where life is great and our emotions are high, or then before we know it, we swing wildly the opposite direction, and we find ourselves in despair. Self-control is when we find our center. It is not the Lord's will for our emotions to swing wildly. Rather, He would have us steady. How can I say that so confidently? Because Scripture teaches: "for God gave us a spirit not of fear but of power and love and self-control" (2 Tim. 1:7).

I had to work hard to find my center, and you will probably have to as well. I had to come to a place where I was not going to allow my emotions to rule the day. I determined that my will and resolve would lead the way, and my emotions would eventually fall into line. Those emotions can be compared to the fuel gauge of a vehicle. The gauge does not tell us where to go. It simply indicates if the tank is full or nearing empty. Emotions do not determine our direction. They are simply an indicator of how we feel, and those feelings can change.

The beautiful part of self-control is that it is a spiritual fruit that God produces in us. Self-control is not gained by our will or strength. It is a fruit that the Holy Spirit desires to produce within us. Therefore, the more we yield to God and allow Him to cultivate that fruit in us, the more self-control we will bear.

Unshakable Assurance

Some mistakenly think that God is a crutch for weak people to lean on. And like a crutch, God is placed into the closet until He is needed again. I would argue that God is not a crutch, but is an unshakable rock that is needed at all times. King David understood this when he wrote: "Lead me to the rock that is higher than I" (Ps. 61:2). I need the steadiness and stability of God. While I confess there have been many times I have found myself fearful and shaking on this rock of Christ Jesus, I have also found that the Rock has never shaken on me. For truly, we have been given "a kingdom that cannot be shaken" (Heb. 12:28). Our assurance comes from confidence in Christ. Anything less is shifting sand.

You do not need physical sight to see God's glory. Just as God has given us five physical senses, the Lord has also given us spiritual senses. This is what Scripture means when it says, "Taste and see that the LORD is good!" (Ps. 34:8). This is what Jesus meant when He said, "He who has ears to hear, let him hear" (Matt. 11:15 ESV). Oddly enough, it is in vision loss that I have seen God the clearest.

As a believer, the question is not whether you have spiritual senses. Indeed, you do have them. The question is whether you are developing them. Spiritual maturity is the development of spiritual senses. A baby has all five senses, but they are not yet developed. There is nothing wrong with being a baby believer as long as you are developing and maturing in your faith. However, Scripture cautions against becoming stagnant in your spiritual growth. Peter teaches: "Like newborn infants, long for the pure spiritual milk, that by it you may grow up into salvation" (1 Pet. 2:2).

People who have an unshakable assurance are not simply lucky. They gain this type of faith as they develop spiritual maturity. As your faith deepens, you will find yourself transitioning from the milk of God's Word to the solid food of Scripture. This is an indication that you are well on your way to a spiritual maturity that cannot be shaken. Note how the author of Hebrews encourages us: "But solid food is for the mature, for those who have their powers of discernment trained by constant practice to distinguish good from evil" (Heb. 5:14).

It is because God has enlightened the eyes of our hearts that we can now see with spiritual sight (Eph. 1:18). It is through these truths that I have learned how to live and enjoy life out of my spirit more so than my physical body. Even though my eyesight has failed, my spiritual vision is clear. The Scripture, "for we walk by faith, not by sight" (2 Cor. 5:7), has taken on a whole new meaning. Although you may not be blind as I am, you, too, can begin to develop your spiritual senses.

Paul teaches: "So we do not lose heart. Though our outer self is wasting away, our inner self is being renewed day by day" (2 Cor. 4:16). When your joy and strength sources from within, you will be able to overcome the areas where your body tries to betray you. I love the word Paul uses for "renewed." The Greek word is *anakainōsis*, where we get our English word *renovation*. The Lord is constantly renovating His people. He is always at work. The question is: Do you trust Him as He works in your life?

Chapter 2

The King's Prison: When Life Isn't Fair

The promise of a new life awaited in Paris. This man grew up poor in Sri Lanka, so when a French family offered to relocate him, he jumped at the opportunity. He was filled with anticipation at the thought of a fresh start in one of Europe's most famous cities. However, this dream quickly turned into a nightmare when their flights connected through Cairo International Airport. Unknowingly to him, the French family had smuggled drugs into luggage that he was helping transport. When someone is caught with drugs in Egypt, they face an automatic twenty-year prison sentence. There are no plea deals or negotiations. There are no time-served ratios or good-behavior deals. It is simply twenty years. When I met this man from Sri Lanka in 2008, he was eighteen years into his twenty-year sentence.

Although I had made many visits to the Al-Qanater Prison, this visit was the first time I had been during Ramadan, the holiest month of the Islamic calendar. As the guards led me down a long corridor, I was shocked to see the number of families that had gathered for their holiday to share a meal with their incarcerated loved ones. I was there for an altogether different reason: to encourage and strengthen persecuted Christians.

A small group of Christian prisoners were in a large holding cell along with Muslim prisoners and their visiting families. I made my way through the crowded room and warmly greeted and hugged my brothers in Christ. Because it was Ramadan, the holding cell was so packed with people, there was nowhere to sit, so we had to remain standing. The noise was deafening. Standing to my left was this man who had been unjustly imprisoned. Through broken English, he shared with me his story. He explained what it was like entering this prison without being able to speak a word of Arabic. He told me how he didn't have a pillow, a blanket, or any hygiene items. In Egypt, families of prisoners provide their basic necessities, and of course, he did not have family in Egypt. He was a lifelong follower of Islam, yet it was his fellow Christian prisoners who shared their food, pillows, blankets, and other necessities with him. This opened his heart to the gospel of Jesus Christ. As he started to tell me how the gospel had transformed his life, he could no longer hold back the emotions. He began sobbing as loudly as anyone I've ever heard weep, and in the most precious broken English I have ever heard, he kept saying, "It has been worth it. It has been worth it to know Christ."

It is in another Egyptian prison that we find one of the most beloved characters of the Bible, Joseph. The chapters spanning his life can be found in Genesis 37–50. The pages of Genesis are packed with remarkable people and stories, from Adam and Eve and the creation account to their sons—Cain who murdered his brother, Abel—to Noah and the global flood. We read about Nimrod and the Tower of Babel, and on to the mighty patriarchs of the faith, from Abraham to Isaac to Jacob. Yet, out of all these extraordinary stories, none captures my attention and stirs my emotions quite like the story of Joseph. Joseph is acquainted with injustice. He was betrayed by his older brothers, sold into slavery against his will, falsely accused of rape, and unjustly thrown into prison.

Each time it seems Joseph has passed God's test, and when it appears that God will reward him, we see God doing the exact opposite. Have you ever felt this way in your own experiences? Perhaps you are someone walking through a season of suffering right now that has left you fearing for the future. The divorce has you reeling. The medical report has you scared. You don't know what tomorrow holds, because you're not sure how you're going to get through today. I think you will relate with the experiences of Joseph. Even though you have tried to live right and be pleasing to the Lord, it seems that circumstances get worse, not better. Just when you think breakthrough is coming to your prayers, it feels like the bottom falls out.

It is important to remember that despite all the things that Joseph endured, his suffering did not last forever, and he always maintained his faith and trust in God. Joseph was seventeen years old when he was sold into slavery (Gen. 37:2), and was thirty when he was promoted to prime minister of Egypt (Gen. 41:46). He died at age 110 (Gen. 50:26). While he endured thirteen long and intense years of suffering, he lived eighty more years blessed and rewarded by God. The point is that time was on his side. So it is with you. Time is on your side as well. How can I say this when I do not know your age nor your circumstance? No matter who you are, you can trust God's plans for your life. I can assure you from the Scriptures that if you belong to the Lord, you will enjoy an eternity without suffering. Paul reminds us: "For this light momentary affliction is preparing for us an eternal weight of glory beyond all comparison" (2 Cor. 4:17). Isn't it interesting how Paul contrasts the words *light* and *momentary* to the concept of *eternal* and *weightiness*? Time was on Joseph's side, and eternity is on your side.

A Dysfunctional Family

Joseph grew up in a dysfunctional environment. Often, when people say they are from a dysfunctional family, I think . . . *Who isn't?* The patriarchs of the faith—Abraham, Isaac, and Jacob—made terrible decisions that brought dysfunction to their homes.

Sarah, the wife of Abraham, tried to solve her inability to conceive by giving her maid, Hagar, to her husband. Hagar conceived and gave birth to Ishmael. Then in their old age, Abraham and Sarah had a son, Isaac. Isaac married Rebecca, who had sons, Esau and Jacob. Isaac loved Esau because he was a man of the earth who loved to hunt, while Rebecca loved Jacob more. Then, Jacob had twelve sons. Unfortunately, he favored and loved Joseph and Benjamin more than his other children because they were the sons of Rachel, whom he loved more than Leah, his first wife. In each situation, favoritism brought suffering upon these family units. Sometimes your suffering is a result of someone else's sin.

Since favoritism ran in the family, it is not surprising that Jacob gave Joseph, his favorite son, a coat of many colors. This fueled his brothers' jealousy. According to Genesis 37, their jealousy had smoldered to the point that the volcano of their emotions erupted. His brothers made a plan to kill him until Reuben, his oldest brother, stepped in to prevent it. Instead, they decided to sell Joseph as a slave, and to lie to their father, telling him that wild animals had killed him. As mentioned above, Genesis 37:2 tells us that Joseph was only seventeen when he was ripped from his home and sold into slavery. This is how he ended up in Egypt.

Arriving in Egypt, Joseph is then sold to Potiphar's house. Some scholars believe that Potiphar may have very well been the chief executioner for Pharaoh himself. Either way, Potiphar had a high position of authority in the Egyptian government. Because Potiphar's job carried so much responsibility, he was rarely home. Genesis 39 describes how Potiphar's wife pursued Joseph day after day, making sexual advances toward him. Because Joseph was a man of conviction, he would not sin against Potiphar, and he would not sin against the Lord (v. 9). This enraged Potiphar's wife.

Potiphar's wife then waited for the right moment when there were no other servants in the house and her husband was gone. She saw her opportunity and tried to lead Joseph to her bedroom. But as she grabbed his garment, he ran from her, leaving his coat in her hands (v. 12). This was the second time that a coat had cost him dearly. Joseph was falsely accused of rape, and like my friend in the opening of the chapter, Joseph found himself in Egypt against his will with very little hope for his future.

The King's Prison

Joseph's life teaches how to respond when God allows us to pass through unfair and undeserved circumstances. Joseph was in prison, but this prison was not an ordinary place. Scripture calls it the king's prison (v. 20). Joseph was exactly where the Lord wanted him. Though his imprisonment was not by his own doing, Joseph was in the will of God. And as with Joseph, God does not randomly place us except by His design. Although life can seem very unfair, how we respond to God and our circumstances will make all the difference.

Certainly, life is not fair, but how do you respond when God seems unfair? It is moments like these I call the king's prison. I entered the king's prison in the fall of 2018 when I went blind. The circumstance of blindness was beyond my control. It was a place I would have never chosen. So many ask me if I feel God has been unfair to me.

It is easy to sometimes feel like God is angry or somehow punishing us, or that we are reaping some kind of divine consequence. However, my friend, Scripture teaches that God walks us through seasons of suffering. When God takes His people through times of suffering, it is not for punishment or without purpose. It is not because God is angry at us. It is because the world is broken, but still He is working a sovereign plan. This is why we must walk by faith and not by sight (2 Cor. 5:7).

Scholars believe that Joseph's stay in an Egyptian prison was most likely underground, with Genesis 40:15 and 41:14 both describing underground as a "pit." How ironic that Joseph's brothers had thrown him into a pit only to be rescued and eventually thrown into an Egyptian pit! Having visited a modern-day Egyptian prison, I can only imagine how cold, dark, and damp an underground Egyptian prison was in Joseph's day.

Are you currently in the king's prison—a place you would have never chosen? Take heart because you are there by God's design. It may feel as though the proverbial rug has been pulled out from beneath you, or that life has thrown you a curveball, but if you belong to the Lord, you are not there by coincidence or bad luck. Even our sufferings are under His sovereign care.

God can step in and turn things around in a moment, but often His rescue is delayed. Many of us have felt this delay. Just when we think God's going to come in and save the day, He doesn't. Just when it seems like our prayers are going to finally break through, they don't, and we find ourselves in a place in life that just doesn't seem fair. Are you there now? There are lessons that only the king's prison can teach us, and if you and I will learn from Joseph that suffering does not last forever, if you and I will pay attention to what God allowed and permitted in his life, it will give us a greater understanding of why God allows us to be in the king's prison.

Lessons in the King's Prison

Wouldn't it have been something if you and I, knowing the end of Joseph's story, could have sat down and had a conversation with him while he was in prison? Maybe it would go something like, "Joseph, chin up. You are not going to believe how God will turn the events of your life. You have no idea what God is preparing you for."

Well, you and I have the benefit of the hindsight of Scripture. Not only do we know the end of Joseph's story, but you and I have promises from God's Word that tell us the end of our story. We know, based upon the promises of Scripture, that "we are more than conquerors through him who loved us" (Rom. 8:37). We know that greater is He who is in us than he who is in the world (1 John 4:4). And we know that God will never leave us nor forsake us (Heb. 13:5). If these verses are true, perhaps we should have a conversation with ourselves and let the still, small voice of the Holy Spirit be the loudest voice we hear. We must let the voice of Scripture speak into our present circumstance.

The king's prison teaches three important principles that should be remembered when suffering hardships:

Principle One: The Lord Was with Joseph

The dominant theme of Genesis 39 is that "the LORD was with Joseph." At least four times, the Holy Spirit reinforces this phrase in the text (vv. 2–3, 21, 23). Whether he was in Potiphar's house or unjustly imprisoned, God never left Joseph's side. Not only did Joseph have God's presence with him, God's "steadfast love" and "favor" were added to him (v. 21). When we look over the entire story of Joseph, we see the providential hand of God at work. The question is: Can we look at our present circumstances and see God's providential hand for us?

As in Joseph's life, "great is his steadfast love toward us, and the faithfulness of the LORD endures forever" (Ps. 117:2). If we pay careful attention, we can sense God's favor amid any present hurt: "For the LORD God is a sun and shield; the LORD bestows favor and honor. No good thing does he withhold from those who walk uprightly" (84:11).

It is comforting to know that the Lord is near to us. Notice that the text does not say Joseph *felt* the Lord near him. It simply says, "The Lord was with Joseph." Though we may not *feel* the Lord near us, it does not change the reality that *He is.* Of course, the Enemy would love for us to feel isolated and abandoned in the king's prison. We can only wonder if Joseph had ever felt abandoned by God.

Shortly after going blind, I faced a severe test when the Enemy tormented me with the thought, "God is light." The Scriptures say there is no darkness in Him at all (1 John 1:5). If this is true, then how can God understand my blindness? How can He know what it is to see only darkness if He is light? These thoughts quickly spiraled into questioning. How could God help me if He could not understand or know what I am experiencing? I knew these thoughts were influenced by Satan, but nonetheless, they had done their damage.

I humbly turned to the Lord and asked Him to help me reconcile the way I felt and what I knew to be true. I will never forget how He graciously answered my prayer. Being new to the king's prison, He took me to Micah 7:8—"Rejoice not over me, O my enemy; when I fall, I shall rise; when I sit in darkness, the LORD will be a light to me." This was the breakthrough I needed and the first spiritual light I saw in my blindness.

We can be assured that no matter the circumstances, the Lord is with us; we are never alone. I live each day confident of God's continual presence with me, and you, too, can walk in that same confidence. Believe that He knows you intimately, He understands, and He sees all.

Are you feeling alone in what you are facing right now? It may be the loss of a job or the loss of a spouse. Perhaps your prodigal children have you doubting God's goodness, or maybe health concerns leave you questioning if God loves you. Regardless of your situation, you are not alone. God sees you. God hears your prayers. God knows your heart. God understands. God has *the* answer.

Principle Two: Look for God's Providence

Who can imagine the daily grind of an underground Egyptian prison? Yet the same favor of God that was with Joseph in his homeland of Canaan was with him at Potiphar's house. Years later, that favor would be with him in the king's prison. The length of Joseph's imprisonment is not known, but Scripture simply states: "They continued for some time in custody" (Gen. 40:4). We know Joseph was sold into slavery at the age of seventeen, and he was promoted by Pharaoh as prime minister of

Egypt at the age of thirty. So, we might suspect that Joseph spent his twenties in the king's prison.

One would think that as the weeks turned into months and then into years, Joseph would have become bitter and resentful, with no hope for release. Then the unthinkable happened. As providence would have it, two of the chief officers of Pharaoh landed in prison with Joseph. Scriptures identify these men as the chief cupbearer and the chief baker. Though we do not know their offenses, we do know Pharaoh was angry with them (Gen. 40:2).

Providence is simply God's involvement. Some people would say it was by chance or coincidence that these two men, who were directly connected to Pharaoh, would be confined with Joseph. But as Christ-followers, we need not rely on the idea of luck: "Nothing whatever, whether great or small, can happen to a believer, without God's ordering and permission. There is no such thing as 'chance,' 'luck,' or 'accident' in the Christian's journey through this world. All is arranged and appointed by God. And all things are 'working together' for the believer's good."[4]

Do you believe God's providential hand orchestrates every detail of your life? It was the godly pastor Alan Redpath who once said, "There is nothing—no circumstance, no trouble, no testing—that can ever touch me until, first of all, it has gone past God and past Christ right through to me. If it has come that far, it has come with a great purpose."[5] If we, like Joseph, can look to the providential hand of God, then what may appear as a random coincidence will begin to look like God's divine plan.

In 1831, no one had ever heard of Abraham Lincoln. He owned a small general store with his business partner, William F. Berry. Standing on the front porch of their failing business, they realized they could not stay afloat much longer. Lincoln said, "It looks as if our business has just about winked out. You know, I wouldn't mind so much if I could just do what I want to do. I want to study law. I wouldn't mind so much if we could sell everything we've got and pay all our bills and have just enough left over to buy one book—*Blackstone's Commentary on English Law*, but I guess I can't."[6]

As providence would have it, about that time a family relocating out west pulled their wagon up to the front of the store. Running out of money, the man offered to sell a barrel to the two businessmen. What use was a barrel when they were about to shut their doors? Berry quickly dismissed him, but Lincoln noticed the countenance of the man's wife. She was near the point of despair. He reached into his vest and gave the man the last fifty cents to his name. Lincoln looked at his business partner and said, "I reckon I could use a good barrel." His business partner was irate. That was all the money they had left, yet Lincoln felt he had done the right thing.

Later that evening, Lincoln noticed something in the bottom of the barrel. He reached in and felt a book. In God's providential care, it was a copy of *Blackstone's Commentary on English Law.*

Providence is God's divine guidance over His creation. Are you sensitive to it? Are you looking for it, even if you feel confined in the king's prison? When the chief butler and chief baker joined Joseph in jail, God's providence was at work. And that day, when a poor family offered Lincoln what appeared to be an empty barrel with little purpose, Lincoln soon recognized God's providential hand in his life. Could it be that God is working divine providence for you?

Principle Three: Serve Others

Picture a bright, sunny day in Egypt. Rather than enjoying the day, you are trapped in the pit of the prison when Joseph asks, "What's wrong? Why are you sad?" (Gen. 40:7). You might wonder if Joseph had lost his mind. He should be angry and jaded. He has every right to be upset and even bitter. However, you see in him a light and faith that believes the truth of God's Word. Despite his dire circumstances, fear and bitterness have not consumed him because he trusts God. For "The LORD is a stronghold for the oppressed, a stronghold in times of trouble. And those who know your name put their trust in you, for you, O LORD, have not forsaken those who seek you" (Ps. 9:9–10).

Are you going through something difficult right now? It might be financial struggles, job issues, health problems, marital difficulties, issues with children, or any other challenge. This is the time to draw close to God, to pray, to seek Him, and to serve Him. This is not the time to back away just because things are not ideal and you see no end to your troubles. Rather, this is when you need God the most. Maybe you are rationalizing that once *you* conquer this difficulty, you will get serious about your relationship with God, but God wants to use your giftings now. God wants to use you in the midst of what you're facing now, not later. It's part of His plan. And thank God that Joseph did not lose sight of his giftings.

People often bargain with God with the hope of getting a desired result. Thankfully, Joseph did not throw his hands up and say, "God, if You want me to interpret another dream, then get me out of prison." We cannot threaten God to achieve our desired results. Our attitude cannot be, "God, if You want me to do something for You, then fix my life." "God, if You want me to serve You, then change my circumstances and answer my prayer." Like Joseph, we must only trust Him to do what is best, aligning our will.

In the early days of blindness, God taught me a valuable lesson about serving others. For whatever reason, I struggled the most on Saturdays. Perhaps it was because this was my primary day off and I was away from the office with less to do, or maybe it was because it was the day before being in the pulpit to proclaim God's Word. Either way, there was a spiritual element to the depression I felt each Saturday. About this time, our church began ministering to the homeless of our city each Saturday evening. We provided a home-cooked meal at a homeless shelter, and while they were hesitant to allow me to preach at first due to too many negative experiences with other churches, we were not discouraged or offended. We continued showing up and getting to know everyone on a first-name basis.

As the weeks and months passed, we eventually built friendships, and the homeless began to open their hearts to us and to the gospel. After a while, they not only allowed us to preach, but they welcomed it with enthusiasm.

I was surprised how much it helped me to serve others on Saturday nights. The very nights I dreaded the most soon became the highlight of my week. Regardless of the hot temperatures in the summer or the bitter cold in the winter, serving the homeless with our team lifted me out of despair.

Many people battle depression, yet one of God's greatest remedies is serving others. When first facing blindness, I wanted to isolate myself. It was easy to become a recluse. I quickly learned that there is a great difference between isolation and solitude. In isolation, you are alone with yourself and your thoughts, which can be self-defeating. Solitude is when you are alone with God, and you are more inclined to pray and listen for His direction and comfort. Isolation breeds depression. Conversely, solitude brings faith and strength through God. When we choose isolation in the king's prison, we overlook others and neglect our gifts. Joseph did not take this path. He served the chief cupbearer and chief baker of Pharaoh, and he willingly used his gift of interpreting dreams. Are we willing to serve others and use our gifts, even though we might be in the king's prison?

When Joseph sees the chief butler and chief baker's countenances, he asks them why they are sad. They respond: "We have had dreams, and there is no one to interpret them" (Gen. 40:8a). These men were used to working in Pharaoh's house where they had access to what the Scriptures call "magicians" (41:8). These are not magicians who merely perform card tricks or illusions. These would have been astrologists, who studied the stars for meaning. Joseph certainly did not attribute his gift to astrology but believed that interpretation came from the Lord (40:8b).

The cupbearer seemed eager to describe his dream, saying, "In my dream there was a vine before me, and on the vine there were three branches. As soon as it budded, its blossoms shot forth, and the clusters ripened into grapes. Pharaoh's cup was in my hand, and I took the grapes and pressed them into Pharaoh's cup and placed the cup in Pharaoh's hand" (vv. 9–11). Joseph gives the interpretation by telling the cupbearer that in three days, he would be restored to his former position.

Then the baker says to Joseph, "I also had a dream: there were three cake baskets on my head, and in the uppermost basket there were all sorts of baked food for Pharaoh, but the birds were eating it out of the basket on my head" (vv. 16–17). This dream's interpretation was not as favorable. Joseph explained that in three days the baker would be executed by Pharaoh.

Joseph, after giving the cupbearer good news, asks, "When you're before Pharaoh, will you remember me? Will you tell him that I'm a Hebrew and I was ripped from my father. I was carried down here against my will, falsely accused, and now I'm in prison. Will you plead my case and help release me?" (see vv. 14–15). Clearly, this reveals that Joseph was human and we, like Joseph, who are in the king's prison, should not think it unrealistic to ask God to change our situation.

We should not feel unspiritual because we want God to change our situation. Do you think I want the Lord to open my eyes? Absolutely, but I am learning a powerful lesson in the king's prison. More than wanting God to change my circumstance, my desire is that He change me. So, I ask you: What are you willing to learn in the king's prison? It is not unspiritual to want your situation to change, but it is unspiritual to throw a temper tantrum because you're there in the first place. God moves, even in the king's prison.

The Making of a Godly Man

How excited do you think Joseph was the day the cupbearer was released? I picture Joseph going back to his cell and collecting his meager belongings. Maybe he took one last look at the wall where he did his best to keep track of the number of days he had been imprisoned. He probably imagined the cupbearer's conversation with the king that would secure his immediate release. But that day didn't come, and it wouldn't come for a long time. Genesis 41:1 is one of the most intriguing verses in the Bible to me. It says, "After two whole years . . ." I cannot shake the word *whole.* Joseph's journey was long, hard, and tedious. Even after interpreting the cupbearer's dream, it was still twenty-four months, and in that time, God continued to make Joseph into a godly man.

Many people who are trapped in the king's prison become restless and question when change will happen. When will God intervene and free them? Maybe as you are reading this, you are frustrated and questioning why you are in the king's prison in the first place. Be assured. God has His timing. It was Pastor Adrian Rogers who said, "With God, timing is far more important than time."[7] "For my thoughts are not your thoughts, neither are your ways my ways, declares the LORD. For as the heavens are higher than the earth, so are my ways higher than your ways and my thoughts than your thoughts" (Isa. 55:8–9).

In our Western culture, we want everything to go according to plan, don't we? We love our calendars. We want everything to follow our schedule, and we want it all to make sense. And we begin to get antsy with God and say, "God, I know I'm here by design. I know I'm here on purpose. I know I'm in the king's prison, but when is it going to change?" God seems to be silent, but His silence does not mean He's not with us. We may doubt and wonder when things will change, but we need not worry. The king's prison is often not a place for us to know just yet, but it is a time to walk by faith and not by sight. It is in this time of waiting, that we say, "Oh God, change me. Change me from the inside out. Lord, mold me into the person You have called me to become."

Fruitful in Afflictions

As noted earlier, Joseph would become the prime minister of Egypt at the age of thirty (Gen. 41:46). He would live to be 110 years old (50:26). This means the next eighty years of his life were greatly rewarded. When his two sons were born, he named them Manasseh and Ephraim. I have a deep appreciation of these names, because it shows that Joseph harbored no bitterness or resentment over the past. He would go on to forgive his brothers and everyone else who had ever wronged him.

Learn from Joseph's example. He was able to move forward in life because he looked past what the hands of men had done and trusted in the providential hand of God. We see this even in the way he named his two sons, with his firstborn being "Manasseh" (to forget). For he said, "God has made me forget all my hardship and all my father's house." The name of the second he called "Ephraim" (to be fruitful): "For God has made me fruitful in the land of my affliction" (41:51–52).

Rather than focusing on the people who have hurt or betrayed you, focus instead on the work God wants to do in your life. God is making crooked ways straight (Eccles. 7:13–14) and producing spiritual fruit out of every hardship we experience, bringing glory to God (John 15:8).

Shortly before Jacob died, he blessed his son Joseph and all his other sons. Consider the blessing he spoke over Joseph: "Joseph is a fruitful vine, a fruitful vine near a spring, whose branches climb over a wall" (Gen. 49:22 NIV). Will you allow your afflictions to produce spiritual fruit in your life? Joseph did, and we can too.

I cannot remember the name of the man from Sri Lanka in the Egyptian prison because from the day we met I called him "Joseph." Although the holding cell was loud and uncomfortable, he asked me to pray over him. I was not prepared for what came next. As I felt the empowerment and enablement of the Holy Spirit, he collapsed into my chest, sobbing great tears of joy. His weeping escalated into wailing, and within moments, the entire holding cell came to a standstill. All eyes were on us, and you could hear a pin drop.

This modern-day Joseph could have grown bitter in his imprisonment but instead, chose to go forward following Jesus.

He was released two years later (two *whole* years later), and he returned home to Sri Lanka as a missionary. With a clear perspective and a mighty calling, sharing the gospel along with his story, many came to know the Lord. It took a while, but God had formed a godly man. So it will be with you and me. God will get His glory, and we will say, "It was worth it!"

Chapter 3

Where Is God in Times of Uncertainty?

On November 12, 2023, Megan Rapinoe, an iconic soccer star, played the last game of her storied career. Yet, it was her comments during the press conference of her last game that struck me the most about her many years in the sport. Only six minutes into her final game, she tore her ACL. Anyone would be disappointed, but she was defiant: *"If there was a God, this is proof that there isn't."* Wherever there is suffering, there is this question: *Where is God?* And for those who haven't learned to see Him even in the suffering, they may find themselves feeling similarly to Rapinoe rather than trusting Him anyway.

This way of thinking is not anything new to humanity. Epicurus, an ancient Greek philosopher who lived 341–270 BC, could not reconcile an all-knowing, all-loving, and all-powerful God with people's experiences of pain. He reasoned: "If God knows about our suffering, cares about our suffering, and can do something about our suffering, then there shouldn't be any suffering!"[8]

The problem is not suffering per se. Most of us understand that we will experience our fair share of it. The real problem is unexplained suffering—painful experiences that God could have prevented or intervened, but for some reason, He doesn't. It is the unexplained suffering of life that threatens to shake our faith.

Unexplained suffering is exactly where Job found himself questioning, *Where is God?* "Behold, I go forward, but he is not there, and backward, but I do not perceive him; on the left hand when he is working, I do not behold him; he turns to the right hand, but I do not see him" (Job 23:8–9). Like most of us, Job judged the actions of God without seeing the full picture. This is why the book of Job is to our benefit. God seems to pull back the curtain to give us a glimpse of what really happens in our seasons of suffering. The aim of this chapter is to lead you beyond the faulty thinking of the Megans and the philosophical reasonings of the Epicuruses of this world and to help you gain healthy, biblical assurance that the trials you face are designed by God for a great purpose.

The Purpose of Job

Most people misunderstand the meaning of the book of Job. Ask ten people what the purpose is, and nine out of ten will say it is to answer the question: *Why do innocent people suffer?* It is a book many turn to when they face difficult situations. Scripture does not leave us to ourselves in trying to figure out the purpose of Job's experiences. It answers it quite definitively in James 5:11—"You have heard of the steadfastness of Job, and you have seen the purpose of the Lord, how the Lord is compassionate and merciful."

It is most often in times of uncertainty or moments of great difficulty that Satan wants us to believe God is nowhere to be found. He wants us to feel as though God has abandoned us and couldn't care less about the disappointments and pain we experience. He would have you believe that God is preoccupied with everyone else, answering their prayers and working miracles in everyone else's life but yours. In other words, he wants you to feel like you are overlooked by God.

The book of Job proves this is not true. James affirms that the purpose of Job's trouble was to show the mercy and compassion of the Lord. If you think Job is only about an innocent man's suffering, this takes God out of the story. You will begin to mistakenly look to yourself for strength and confidence, and you will be greatly disappointed if you look to others as Job did his three friends. We must only look to the Lord. As King David said, "I lift up my eyes to the hills. From where does my help come? My help comes from the LORD, who made heaven and earth" (Ps. 121:1–2).

Scholars believe that Job is the oldest book of the Bible. We know that Job lived 140 years after Satan brought calamity upon his life and God returned his fortunes (Job 42:16). He was probably around sixty years old when chapter 1 opens, because he was established and wealthy and all ten of his children were in adulthood. It is safe to suppose that Job lived approximately two hundred years. This would have put him around the time of Abraham and in the post-flood era. Abraham's father lived to be 205 (Gen. 11:32), which would be consistent with Job's lifespan.[9] Another reason scholars believe Job would've been contemporaries with Abraham or his father is because Job is one of the few biblical books that predates the Law and the Levitical priesthood under Moses.

As we explore the life of Job together, keep in mind Lamentations 3:31–33: "For the Lord will not cast off forever, for, though he cause grief, he will have compassion according to the abundance of his steadfast love; for he does not afflict from his heart or grieve the children of men." There was purpose to Job's suffering, and there is purpose in your painful times as well. God is not acting randomly in your life. Instead, He is consistent with His character, which is love (1 John 4:8).

A Snapshot

There are many surprises in the first two chapters of Job. It surprises me that Satan is so active in the story. He is both walking the earth, as well as presenting himself before God in heaven. It surprises me even more that Satan completely fades from the narrative after chapter 2. This indicates that while Satan is active, the story is really about God, not Satan. What surprises me above all, though, is that it was God who first challenged Satan with the integrity of Job. Job 1:1–4 gives us a snapshot of Job's life. According to verse 1 he was, "blameless and upright, one who feared God and turned away from evil." This does not imply that he was sinless, but he was certainly a righteous man (Ezek. 14:14).

Not only was Job a spiritual man, but he was also a good family man. Job 1:2 says he had seven sons and three daughters.

His children often feasted on "their day," most likely meaning their birthday, and Job would make sacrifices for each of them in case they inadvertently cursed God. Since this is before the time of priestly and Levitical sacrifices, Job acted as a priest to his family, representing them before the Lord.

This snapshot shows us a spiritual man, a family man, but also a powerful man with great wealth. In those days, wealth was measured by livestock. So great was his wealth that according to verse 3 (CSB) he was "the greatest man . . . of the east."

Behind the Scenes

The story takes an interesting twist with Job 1:6—"Now there was a day when the sons of God came to present themselves before the LORD, and Satan also came among them." Who exactly are these sons of God? Throughout the Scriptures, the term "sons of God" refers to the ranks of angels (Gen. 6:1–4; Job 1:6; 2:1; 38:7). Satan is among this group because he was a created angel (Ezek. 28:14). Jesus said that He saw Satan fall as "lightning from heaven" (Luke 10:18).

The sin of pride and rebellion caused Satan to lose his position in heaven. Isaiah 14:13–16 depicts Satan saying, "I will" against God five times: "'I will ascend to heaven; above the stars of God I will set my throne on high; I will sit on the mount of assembly in the far reaches of the north; I will ascend above the heights of the clouds; I will make myself like the Most High.' But you are brought down to Sheol, to the far reaches of the pit. Those who see you will stare at you and ponder over you."

Although Satan has lost his position as an angel, he still has access to the throne of God. His role today is to be an "accuser" (Rev. 12:10) and "adversary" (1 Pet. 5:8) of God's people. In Job 1, we find Satan walking the earth. After all, he is "the god of this world" (2 Cor. 4:4) and "the prince of the power of the air" (Eph. 2:2). For now, he has access to God's throne, but that will one day change as he will be permanently kicked out of heaven (Rev. 12).

Once Satan is kicked out of heaven, he will go to war with Michael, the archangel. Contrary to what many believe, Christ and Satan are not rivals, and they are especially not co-equals. Christ is the Creator of angels and worshiped by them (Heb. 1:6). This means Satan and everything else is created by Christ. "For by him all things were created, in heaven and on earth, visible and invisible, whether thrones or dominions or rulers or authorities—all things were created through him and for him" (Col. 1:16).

Furthermore, when Satan will one day be bound, it is not Christ who binds him, nor is it even an archangel. Revelation 20:1 simply identifies him as "an angel coming down from heaven." That a mere low-ranking angel can carry this out beautifully depicts the power of God over the power of our Enemy.

As we return to the story, God asks Satan if he has "considered" his servant Job (Job 1:8). Does it shock you that Job wasn't on Satan's radar? It was God who mentioned him first, showing His control of the situation. Satan responds to the Lord: "Does Job fear God for no reason? Have you not put a hedge around him and his house and all that he has, on every side? You have blessed the work of his hands, and his possessions have increased in the land. But stretch out your hand and touch all that he has, and he will curse you to your face" (vv. 9–11).

God then does the unthinkable. He grants Satan permission to disturb Job's life: "And the LORD said to Satan, 'Behold, all that he has is in your hand. Only against him do not stretch out your hand.' So Satan went out from the presence of the LORD" (v. 12). Satan wasted no time. Job received four back-to-back messengers who announced terrible calamity. First, Satan wiped out his wealth through thieves that raided his livestock and fire that consumed the rest. Then, he lost all ten of his children to a windstorm that collapsed the house where they were dining. In a single day, Job lost everything but his health (vv. 13–19).

Satan's Challenge and Job's Response

In all this calamity, Satan's challenge was that Job would curse God: "But stretch out your hand and touch all that he has, and he will curse you to your face" (v. 11). Cursing God seemed to be a primary concern for Job. Remember, this is why he offered sacrifices on his children's behalf in case they inadvertently cursed God in their hearts (v. 5). Even Job's exasperated wife tells him to "curse God and die" (2:9). When you consider how high the stakes were and that Job had no knowledge of the conversation between God and Satan, it is even more astounding that he never cursed God. In fact, Scripture says, "In all this Job did not sin or charge God with wrong" (1:22).

A key to understanding how Job weathered this calamity is found in Job 1:20. He "fell on the ground and worshiped." What a way to respond to afflictions! Job did not blame the thieves who raided his livestock, and he did not blame God for the wind that took his children's lives. Instead, he fell down and worshiped. While this isn't usually the first response that comes to mind, I had the opportunity to see this in action.

A young man had begun attending my church when his little girl was first born. She was about six months old when he was killed in a tragic car accident. Shepherding this family, I had a front-row seat to how they responded to this crushing hurt. I watched his wife, a new widow with an uncertain future, resolve to live for the Lord and raise her daughter for God's glory. I watched his parents bear the weight of burying their son. While I helped his mother pick out the casket, she physically fainted. Yet at his memorial service, she worshiped God in a way unlike I had ever seen.

At the graveside, I reminded the family of an old Puritan saying: When a flower is crushed, it releases the gift of its fragrance. I watched this family do exactly that. When their loss crushed them, they became the aroma of Christ. Perhaps you find yourself in a season of suffering. Job gives us a remarkable example to follow. Are you able to worship God no matter what touches your life?

Satan was convinced if he brought disaster upon Job, he would curse God to His face. Yet, worship seems to put things in the right perspective. Rather than cursing God, Job says, "Naked I came from my mother's womb, and naked shall I return. The

LORD gave, and the LORD has taken away; blessed be the name of the LORD" (v. 21). Can you imagine what Satan thought when Job said, "blessed be the name of the Lord"? It is the same when you worship in the midst of your suffering. Rather than blaming God, Job worshiped him. Instead of growing bitter away from God, Job went toward him. We have the same choice.

It would be great if chapter 1 was the end of Job's testing, but it was far from over. In chapter 2, Satan approaches God once again: "But stretch out your hand and touch his bone and his flesh, and he will curse you to your face" (v. 5). Once again, God grants Satan permission. This time, he can afflict Job's health, save only to spare his life.

At this point, Job's wife seemingly encourages him to "curse God and die" (v. 9). People often speak very poorly of his wife, but we must remember, she lost as much as Job did, and no doubt was overwhelmed with grief. Job's response to his wife's grief is stunning. Note that he did not call her a foolish woman, but said that she spoke, "as one of the foolish women would speak." He then explains to her, "Shall we receive good from God, and shall we not receive evil?" (v. 10a).

Once again, Satan thought Job would curse God, and now his wife is encouraging him to do so. Yet, "In all this Job did not sin with his lips" (v. 10b). Job taught me one of the greatest ways to pray. In my own experience with blindness, I, too, want to be careful that I do not sin with my lips. We can pray the words of Job 40:4—"Behold, I am of small account; what shall I answer you? I lay my hand on my mouth." When I do not understand why God is leading me through this valley of darkness, my favorite way to pray is to cover my mouth with my hand and to say in my heart, "You are God, and I am not." The next time you struggle to pray, rather than doing all the talking, sit quietly before the Lord and, as a gesture of faith, like Job, cover your mouth with your hand and let God be God.

Searching for God

At times, I must work hard to find my center. After going blind, I have found that the pendulum of my emotions can swing wildly. There are some days I am so productive that by the end of the day, I have forgotten that I am blind. Of course, there are other days when it's a struggle to get out of bed. As mentioned before, I used to struggle the most after vivid dreams. I cannot entirely tell you what it is like to dream in full color and see familiar faces, only to wake up to everything pitch-black. I cannot see any light, no matter how bright it is. I can look directly into the sun, feel its warmth, but see no light at all. It is in these moments of defeat I have found myself searching for God. It's in the uncertainty, even when God feels a million miles away, that we find God and that we often find ourselves as well. Yet, God values authenticity, even when it surfaces questions we have about Him. Some of the most moving passages in the book of Job are the gut-wrenching, soul-searching dialogues with the Almighty. It is remarkable that God has preserved these conversations for His people.

Beginning in Job 2, we are introduced to three of his friends, Eliphaz, Bildad, and Zophar. Many of their conversations quickly turn into accusations. It is worth noting that there is not one incident recorded where Job's friends prayed for him. Instead, their primary argument to Job is that he was suffering because of his sins. This could not be further from the truth, with chapters 1 and 2 affirming he was a blameless and upright man.

We must be careful which voices we allow to speak into our life. Just because someone is a friend does not mean their advice is godly or even wise. Job spent a great deal of time listening to his friends, and it caused him more grief and frustration. His friends continue to challenge his integrity and righteousness, and when we come to chapter 23, bitterness is beginning to set in:

> "Today also my complaint is bitter;
> my hand is heavy on account of my groaning.
> Oh, that I knew where I might find him,
> that I might come even to his seat!
> I would lay my case before him
> and fill my mouth with arguments.
> I would know what he would answer me
> and understand what he would say to me.
> Would he contend with me in the greatness of
> his power?
> No; he would pay attention to me.
> There an upright man could argue with him,
> and I would be acquitted forever by my judge.
>
> "Behold, I go forward, but he is not there,
> and backward, but I do not perceive him;

> on the left hand when he is working, I do not
> behold him;
> he turns to the right hand, but I do not see
> him." (vv. 2–9)

Can you feel the pressure Job is under? His wife is drowning in her own grief and encouraging him to "curse God and die" (v. 9). His friends are accusing him and tearing him down rather than building him up. Above all, God is nowhere to be found. We all struggle with this from time to time. We can take comfort in David's words: "For he knows our frame; he remembers that we are dust" (Ps. 103:14). Do not let Satan tell you that God is angry with you. "As a father shows compassion to his children, so the LORD shows compassion to those who fear him" (v. 13).

He Knows My Way

For all of Job's questions and complaints, he knew what we often forget: God knows what He is doing. "He knows the way that I take; when he has tried me, I shall come out as gold" (Job 23:10). This verse is so meaningful to me personally, because it tells me that the path God has me on is not random nor coincidental. It is a path He has chosen. When you come to the realization that God is our Shepherd and He leads us in "paths of righteousness," you will not fear what lies ahead (Ps. 23:1, 3–4). Instead, you will say, "Lord, do in me what You deem good and necessary."

Does your heart need reassuring that God sees the path you are on? Although Job did not sense God near him, he still trusted Him. We can live by this same kind of faith. A few months before losing complete eyesight, I was so afraid of walking the path of blindness. One night I was lying in bed and Sadie thought I was asleep, but I was pouring out my heart and telling God every fear I had about being blind, and while some of those deepest fears have come true, I have never walked one moment of it alone. This is Job's strength to walk a path of suffering, and it can be yours as well: You do not walk alone. God knows our way, because, as John Piper notes, our Shepherd is not behind us pushing us forward, but is in front of us, leading us on paths where He has walked every step we are to take.[10] The path God has you on may have you perplexed, but be assured, He is trustworthy. Often, God sets our feet on "crooked" paths (Eccles. 7:13). The Puritans explained why. They reasoned it is only when we are walking on crooked paths that we must train our eyes on the Lord. Do not despise where the Lord has you, because it is not by accident, but for a great purpose.[11]

The Refiner's Fire

Job continues to affirm his faith by saying, "when he has tried me, I shall come out as gold" (Job 23:10). Notice how he does not mention Satan, nor his three friends. Job looked past Satan's hand and the distraction of others, and focused on the sovereign hand of God. It is so easy to blame others for our lot in life. It is easy for Christians to blame Satan for everything that goes wrong. Job didn't do this, but trusted that God was transforming him. Many have asked me if I blame the doctor who tore my retina. My answer is always the same: *Absolutely not.* I can say this because of what I've learned from Job. He understood it was God and God alone taking him through the refiner's fire.

God is seen as a Refiner throughout the Scriptures (Job 23:10; Mal. 3:2–3; Zech. 13:9; 1 Pet. 1:7; 4:12). The process of refining gold has not changed much through the centuries. The only way to make gold pure is with intense heat. To be purified, the rock, dirt, and grime must be melted away with intense heat. Real gold is never affected by the fire. As the gold is refined, the dross rises to the top. Do you know when the refiner knows the gold has been made pure? It is when he scrapes off the dross and can see his reflection in the gold. This is a beautiful picture of our times of testing.

Is it any wonder Peter wrote to suffering saints: "Beloved, do not be surprised at the fiery trial when it comes upon you to test you, as though something strange were happening to you" (1 Pet. 4:12)? As you consider the difficulties of your life and wonder why God is allowing them, remember that it is "so that the tested genuineness of your faith—more precious than gold that perishes though it is tested by fire—may be found to result in praise and glory and honor at the revelation of Jesus Christ" (1:7).

A book that has sustained my faith through my own Refiner's fire testing has been the classic devotional *Streams in the Desert.* Allow me to share from it this beautiful poem on the Refiner's fire:

He sat by a fire of seven-fold heat,
As He watched by the precious ore,
And closer He bent with a searching gaze
As He heated it more and more.
He knew He had ore that could stand the test,
And He wanted the finest gold
To mould as a crown for the King to wear,
Set with gems with a price untold.

So He laid our gold in the burning fire,
Tho' we fain would have said Him "Nay,"
And He watched the dross that we had not seen,
And it melted and passed away.
And the gold grew brighter and yet more bright,
But our eyes were so dim with tears,
We saw but the fire—not the Master's hand,
And questioned with anxious fears.

Yet our gold shone out with a richer glow,
As it mirrored a Form above,
That bent o'er the fire, tho' unseen by us,
With a look of ineffable love.

Can we think that it pleases His loving heart
To cause us a moment's pain?
Ah, no! but He saw through the present cross
The bliss of eternal gain.

So He waited there with a watchful eye,
With a love that is strong and sure,

And His gold did not suffer a bit more heat
Than was needed to make it pure . . .[12]

Questions Answered

Throughout the book of Job, we see him puzzled as to why God allowed such calamity in his life. We have seen him affirm his faith by recognizing God is taking him through the Refiner's fire. Still, Job is faced with God's seeming silence and absence. To Job's amazement, God finally answers him. The Almighty asks Job a series of seventy-seven questions to which Job has no answer.

By the time we reach the final chapter of Job, he sees everything, including God, in a new light: "Then Job answered the Lord and said: 'I know that you can do all things, and that no purpose of yours can be thwarted'" (Job 42:1–2). Job saw correctly that the purpose of his story was ultimately about God. Oh, that you and I would have the same perception of God. Second, Job also saw himself through a different lens: "'Who is this that hides counsel without knowledge?' Therefore I have uttered what I did not understand, things too wonderful for me, which I did not know. 'Hear, and I will speak; I will question you, and you make it known to me.' I had heard of you by the hearing of the ear" (vv. 3–5a).

All that Job encountered led him to where God wants to lead us—to repentance. Remember in Job 1:20 that when calamity began, he worshiped God. But in Job 42:6, we see him repenting. This is the greatest sign of yielding and submitting oneself to God. In the end, Job repented for doubting God's goodness and questioning His sovereignty. From the very beginning, he had faith to worship God without seeing His full plan. He went from having conversations with his friends to having a dialogue with God Himself. It was in his conversations with the Lord that his faith deepened and matured.

God also dealt with Job's three friends. To their credit, they repented and obeyed the Lord as well (Job 42:7–9). Yet there is a key concept that is often overlooked in Job. According to Job 42:10, it is when Job prayed for his three friends that God turned everything around. Job's ability to forgive was the key that unlocked God's favor: "And the LORD restored the fortunes of Job, when he had prayed for his friends. And the LORD gave Job twice as much as he had before."

Just as God sat out to restore all that Job had lost, so He will do for you as well. God does not waste anything, especially our pain. You may not be able to see the full plan of God yet. You may only have a few pieces to the puzzle, but rest assured, God is working His plan for you, and He will restore you, even if not on this side of eternity. Job still grieved his losses; restoration does not mean erasing the pain of the past, but it does bring comfort and hope for new days.

Just as Job 1 and 2 pull back the curtain to show us the conversation between God and Satan, so God pulls back the curtain to reveal the plans He has for you: "For I know the plans I have for you, declares the LORD, plans for welfare and not for evil, to give you a future and a hope" (Jer. 29:11). This good news was delivered in a long stint of suffering for God's people—seventy years of exile in Babylon, to be exact. It would be slow and it would be painful. Some who received this promise would never see its fulfillment. But still, God's plan is good because God's plan is for suffering to be no more through the power of Jesus for all of eternity. It may be a while. It was a while for Job and it was a while for the exiled Israelites, but God will restore.

The book ends by saying that "Job died, an old man, and full of days" (Job 42:17). What is going to be the end of our story? It will end like Job's with God sovereign and Satan defeated, and all things working together for our eternal good.

Chapter 4

Holy Ground

Michael received a message at 9:30 p.m. on January 31, 2024, while watching a movie with his fiancée, Taylor. A friend's wife said, "My husband is acting irrationally. I need you guys here now." His fiancée encouraged him to go, as two veterans he had served with had taken their own lives the previous week, and he hoped to prevent a third loss. He and two friends rushed to the home to see how they could help. Little did Michael know that his life was about to change forever.

The husband was extremely agitated, and Michael tried talking to him to find out how he could help. His friend said he needed to go for a walk to calm down. Minutes later, Michael heard a door being kicked. He slipped behind a hallway door, seeing through the gap the man holding a gun. The next thing Michael heard were shots being fired, and the first bullet struck in his head, ripping through his left eye, sinus cavity, and out his right cheek. The first gunshot wound left him completely blind. When the man realized Michael was still alive, he shot him a second time in the chest. When first responders reached him, they found him lying in a pool of blood, trying to stem his own wounds.

Miraculously, Michael survived that night. When he reached the ER, they began to prepare him for emergency surgery. There happened to be a ballistics trauma surgeon on call that was waiting to receive him when the ambulance arrived at the hospital. The doctors and nurses were shocked he hadn't lost consciousness during the entire ordeal, a credit to his vast military training. Since he had refused any pain medication that might affect his ability to stay awake, he was in unbearable pain by the time they started prepping for surgery. At this point in Michael's life, to say he was away from God would be an understatement. He was living life on his own terms, and God was nowhere in his thoughts or plans.

As the pain increasingly became unbearable, Michael later recalled that a man entered the surgical room and placed his hands on his shoulders. Michael testifies that he had never felt a strength like he felt in the man's hands, yet they were gentle at the same time. It brought such peace to him that he was able to lie still until the scans could be completed. The man said, "Rest. I am here with you, and I will be here when you wake up."

Suffering so much blood loss caused Michael's heart to go into cardiac arrest. After a minute and a half of chest compressions, his heart began to beat again. Michael underwent a total of four surgeries over a three-day period. When he woke up in the ICU, he was completely blind and without a gallbladder, spleen, and four feet of intestines—but he was alive. The doctors were unable to come up with any medical explanation for how Michael survived. They said his chance of survival was less than 10 percent. Surgeons said he would most likely be in the ICU for two months, but after only eight days, he walked out of the hospital.

About a week later, he said to his fiancée, "I'm pretty sure I saw an angel in the hospital." She describes Michael as extremely scientific and analytical, so to say this was shocking to her is an understatement. Whether this was a man on call in the operating room or truly an interaction with an angel is impossible to know, but try convincing Michael otherwise. This experience moved Michael to spend his recovery time deep in thought with a new commitment to listen to an audio Bible. He realized that even though he had an experience with God, who had sustained his life, he had not yet surrendered his life to Him. So, on March 17, 2024, Michael prayed and gave his life to the Lord, and today I get to worship with Michael every Sunday. During the weeks of recovery, you can imagine how their lives were reeling. They were hungry for spiritual guidance. Taylor decided to google "Blind Pastor," and that is how they found me. Soon after, we connected by email and then phone, and it wasn't long until they were visiting me in Tennessee. Eventually, God called them to relocate, and now I have the joy of worshiping with Michael and Taylor each Sunday.

The Desert Experience

Like my friend Michael, Moses lived life on his own terms until God got his attention. Moses was eighty years old when God appeared to him in the desert of Midian. How he ended up in Midian is a fascinating tale of its own. Although destined for greatness, when we find Moses in Midian, he is a broken man, filled with regret and living in obscurity. His life had not turned out anything like he had imagined. He was raised with every social, political, and financial advantage anyone could have been given. He grew up in the palaces of Egypt, the adopted son of Pharaoh's daughter, and the adopted grandson of Pharaoh himself. He received the finest education with the brightest of Egyptian minds.

But there's more to the story. God was at work in Moses's life. Although he grew up as a member of Pharaoh's family, Moses was born as a Hebrew and never lost sight of his heritage. At the time of his birth, Pharaoh had ordered the slaughter of every Hebrew male child under the age of two. Moses's mother would not hear of it. By faith, she took Moses to the Nile River, placed him in a woven basket, and released him into the providential care of God.

Amazingly, Moses ended up where Pharaoh's daughter was bathing. When she heard the baby crying, she rescued him from the dangerous waters and adopted him as her own. What's more amazing is that Miriam, the older sister of Moses, followed along the riverbank, keeping a watchful eye on her brother. She approached Pharaoh's daughter and offered her mother's services to nurse and wean the child. Thus, God providentially allowed Moses to grow up with his birth family and under the influence of Hebrew culture.

Over time, it became more and more difficult for him to watch his people suffer at the hands of the Egyptians. By the time Moses was forty years old, he could no longer turn a blind eye or a deaf ear to their afflictions. "By faith Moses, when he was grown up, refused to be called the son of Pharaoh's daughter, choosing rather to be mistreated with the people of God than to enjoy the fleeting pleasures of sin" (Heb. 11:24–25). One day, he sprang into action, when, in horror, he watched an Egyptian taskmaster beating a fellow Israelite. He struck the Egyptian down, killing and burying him. In that moment, Moses went from Egyptian royalty to a sought-after fugitive. This is how he ended up in the desert of Midian.

In our spiritual walk, we each go through desert experiences. These are difficult times; God seems distant, our prayer life seems dry, and we struggle with doubts and questions. Yet it is in these desert experiences when God does His work of preparation. A. W. Tozer once said, "It is doubtful whether God can bless a man greatly until He has hurt him deeply."[13] Indeed, God would use Moses in a great way, but not until He first prepared him in the desert.

Notice how Exodus 3:1 pinpoints his location. Like a spiritual Google Map, the Holy Spirit tells us that Moses was on the "west side of the wilderness." While we all go through desert experiences, it is another thing to find ourselves on the "backside of the desert," as the King James Version calls it—a place of isolation, uncertainty, and regret. Yet this is where Moses was. You cannot get any more remote than the back side of a wilderness. What I hear in this passage is that Moses is as isolated as he can be, and moreover, he wants it that way.

Isolation is dangerous for any believer. As mentioned in chapter 2, God does His best work in solitude, while Satan does his best work in isolation. Isolation is an unhealthy space. Have you ever found yourself on the back side of a spiritual wilderness? Do you know what it is like to want to hide away and be left alone? Moses did, and yet all along, God was working.

Moses's time spent in the back side of a wilderness was not entirely wasted time, because he was leading the flock of his father-in-law, Jethro (Exod. 3:1). This is a significant change for Moses. Remember that Moses grew up a prince of Egypt and a promising leader. He was part of the royal family of Pharaoh. Now, he is working as a shepherd, one of the lowliest occupations in biblical times.

Perhaps Moses thought his life was over. He had seen dreams shattered and hopes dashed. He likely doubted his decision to leave his comfortable life in Egypt. One might wonder how many days Moses ate his meager lunch among his small flock of sheep, thinking about the finest foods from Pharaoh's house. Those days of greatness were gone, and now all he had to look forward to was tending sheep in the desert conditions. Little did Moses know that God was doing some of His best work in those long, drawn-out days in Midian. Moses, who now led a small flock of sheep, would soon be called to lead over one million Israelites out of the land of Egypt into the land of Canaan.

A Man on the Run

Moses's crimes meant he had to put as much distance as possible between himself and Egypt, becoming a man on the run. Midian was a distance of some three hundred miles from

Egypt. It was located in the southern Sinai mountains in what is today the Hijaz area of Jordan and northwest Saudi Arabia, near the Red Sea coast. He lived the next forty years looking over his shoulder, fearing that the Egyptian authorities would catch up to him. The Lord confirms this when He commands him to go back to Egypt. This time, however, He assures him, "All the men who were seeking your life are dead" (Exod. 4:19).

Satan will try to increase our appetites for the comforts of Egypt, and when that doesn't work, he'll make us feel like we have failed and need to enter the back side of the desert in a place of obscurity and regret. Both of these vices will make us ineffective. Yet what Moses's life teaches us is that God meets us in our mistakes and failures, and continues His planned assignment for our lives. You may be in the desert, but you are not hidden from the Lord's sight. Are you trying to hide? Are you running from someone or something, or even from God? It is exhausting to run from God, and quite pointless since He sees you just as clearly as He saw Moses on the back side of the desert. And in this, He has not come to condemn you, but to restore you through the power of Christ. "There is therefore now no condemnation for those who are in Christ Jesus" (Rom. 8:1).

For Moses, God's call to him came out in this desert through a flame within a bush. When God spoke to him out of the blazing bush, he said, "Moses, Moses!" Moses replied, "Here I am" (Exod. 3:4). The man who tried so hard to hide had been found. God did not reveal Himself to condemn Moses, but so that He might restore Moses and bless His people through him.

God Who Pursues

And in this approach of God to Moses, we find what sets Christianity apart from all other faiths. In other world religions, we find man seeking after a God, but in biblical faith, we see God seeking after man. Ultimately, we have Christ leaving the comforts of heaven to dwell with us—as "Emmanuel," God with us—which is a pursuit like no other. How extraordinary it is to think that a man like Moses, who was not looking for God, was still pursued and found by God, seen in a fire. The word *blaze* when used as a verb means "to burn brightly." The greatest need of today is a church ablaze, because fire always attracts. When God revealed Himself to Moses, He did so through fire, drawing him out of his isolation.

Throughout the entirety of the Scriptures, God uses fire to symbolize His presence. When John the Baptist introduced Jesus to the world, he said, "I baptize you with water for repentance, but he who is coming after me is mightier than I, whose sandals I am not worthy to carry. He will baptize you with the Holy Spirit and fire" (Matt. 3:11). It is no different in the church today. Since the presence of God dwells among us, we are called to be "the light of the world" (Matt. 5:14).

Christians sometimes think of the terms *Holy Spirit* and *fire* as emotional experiences, yet the fire of God is not emotionalism nor sensationalism. Holy fire is to be experienced by every believer. Because I pastor a nondenominational church, I have the joy, and sometimes challenge, of interacting with believers from various denominational backgrounds. What I often find is that we are prone to define and label certain biblical ideas based on the lens of our previous church experiences, rather than a biblical lens. For example, when we began a weekly prayer meeting, it was different than what most people expected. Why? Because their expectations were based on previous experiences. Different churches have different styles and preferences. Biblical truth transcends these. So it is with the idea of the Holy Spirit and fire. We must be careful that we define these biblical truths based on Scripture.

What is holy fire? It is a passionate zeal and a burning desire for the glory of God. It is a cleansing flame that will burn out sins and impurities. When the Holy Spirit fell upon the first believers in Acts 2, He came as a mighty, rushing wind and a flame of fire. If they needed it then, how much more so do we need it today?

As a teen, I had seen God work in and through me, but I wanted more. For weeks, I asked the Lord to fill my life with His presence and to show me what was lacking. One day, while I was at school, a snowstorm came while my parents were at work, so I rode home with my neighbor. I planned to spend the day at their house, but I kept sensing the Lord wanted me to go home, even though no one was there. As I obeyed His prompting, I felt the Lord wanted me to pray. It was in that moment, alone in my room, that I felt the holy fire of God come into my soul—a fire that set the course for my life and that has never been quenched. This fiery desire for Him was only from Him, and it helped me understand what Jeremiah meant when he wrote: "There is in my heart as it were a burning fire shut up in my bones" (Jer. 20:9).

When I planted Preaching Christ Church at the age of twenty, I was feeling the stress and pressure of starting a church from nothing. We had no financial backing, no outside support, and only a handful of people. Each week was a struggle. One weekend, a family I had never met showed up at church out of nowhere. They only attended that one service, but they handed me a note that I still have to this day. It said, "Do not be discouraged. While you were preaching, we saw stacks of smoke, and the Lord said He is going to set you on fire and people will come to watch you burn." When God pursues you and purifies you with His fire, you, too, will be set ablaze for the world to see, no matter what situation you face. This was God's intention with Moses, that he would experience God in the flame and be ready to face whatever assignment God gave him. He saw the fire, and he stood on holy ground, the place that God reveals Himself and calls us to a life not defined by our sufferings or our past, but by His power.

Holy Ground

When the Lord revealed Himself by fire and captured Moses's attention, He said, "Take your sandals off your feet, for the place on which you are standing is holy ground" (Exod. 3:5). Midian was located between present-day Jordan and Saudi Arabia, a remote area that represented a place of obscurity, failure, and regret. Yet God called it holy ground. No matter your sufferings, regrets, or mistakes, God can redeem all of it. I could dwell on the disappointment of losing eyesight, or I could see it as holy ground. You can choose bitterness and resentment over whatever you have lost, or you can allow God to turn it into holy ground.

Mount Horeb was an ordinary place. There was nothing holy about it up to that point. So, what made it holy ground? The presence of God. And so it is with us; God makes us holy because Christ dwells in our hearts by faith (Eph. 3:17). This is what enables us to "present [our] bodies as a living sacrifice, holy and pleasing to God; this is [our] true worship" (Rom. 12:1 CSB).

Holy means set apart. When we are on holy ground, we experience the transformational power of the gospel. It is when the flesh begins to give way to the Spirit (Rom. 7:4–6). This is what it means to be born again. We become a new creation in Christ; the old passes away and the new comes to life (2 Cor. 5:17). After we are new and born again, we then have God's Spirit within us, which changes who we are and what we desire. Thus, our nature changes. This is why 1 Peter 1:15–16 enjoins us: "But as he who called you is holy, you also be holy in all your conduct, since it is written, 'You shall be holy, for I am holy.'" Our children are like us because they were born of us and have our nature. Likewise, when we are born again, we take on God's way of thinking, His characteristics, and His way of living.

Lastly, God told Moses to take off his sandals since he was standing on holy ground. Why was he commanded to take off his shoes? In short, we cannot approach God on our own terms. We may be naturally gifted and highly talented, but we cannot draw near to God with talent only. We may excel and outperform in our work life, but we cannot approach God with pride. We must remove these things if we are to experience holy fire on holy ground.

When God Gets Our Attention

Hearing the call of God from a burning bush captured Moses's full attention, as he removed his shoes and carefully listened. Not much captures our full attention today with our tiny screens always in hand, but our lives would look quite different if every day we chose to give our full attention to God. Up to this point in his life, Moses did not know God. He may have heard stories from his mother and the other Hebrews, but he did not know God personally until the Lord revealed Himself as the God of Abraham, Isaac, and Jacob. Although this would be the first time Moses encountered the Lord, it certainly would not be the last. With his full attention on God, he'd be used to write the first five books of the Old Testament. He'd receive the Ten Commandments and the Law, as well as the tabernacle design and all the sacrifices, ceremonies, and holidays of Israel. Once his full attention was given to God at the burning bush, God not only used Moses mightily, acting as God's mouthpiece among Israel and His deliverer, bringing God's people out of Egypt. God also created a unique and eternal friendship with Moses: "Thus the LORD used to speak to Moses face to face, as a man speaks to his friend" (Exod. 33:11). Not only does God use those whose full attention is on Him, He also creates a friendship with the Almighty. Jesus said that God no longer calls us servants, but friends (John 15:15). This friendship between God and Moses is eternal, because God still has plans to use Moses in the last days. When Moses died, the Lord Himself hid his body, yet this was not the end of his story (Deut. 34:5–6). Moses and Elijah appeared with Christ on the Mount of Transfiguration. In each account of the Gospels, it states that Christ, Moses, and Elijah had a conversation, but only the Gospel of Luke tells us what they talked about. Moses and Elijah speak about Christ; namely, "of his departure, which he was about to accomplish at Jerusalem" (Luke 9:31). It is very possible that their conversation entailed not only the imminent death of Christ, but also end-time events foretold in the Bible. My personal belief is that the two witnesses of Revelation 11 will be Moses and Elijah. That day when God captured Moses's attention, his life was changed and would alter the history of Israel and the unfolding plans of God into eternity.

Few people experience God's presence the way Moses did. He relied so much on God's presence that he told the Lord that he would not take Israel any further unless God assured them His presence would go with them (Exod. 33:15). Do you value the presence of God the way Moses did? God is as eager to speak to you and to walk with you through every high and low of life as He was Moses. It is not that God is unable to speak. It is that we are often unwilling to listen. When we begin to long for God's presence, He will begin to speak. Let your heart's cry be the same as the psalmist: "As a deer pants for flowing streams, so pants my soul for you, O God" (Ps. 42:1).

Suffering Is a Gift

When Michael was shot by a friend and permanently lost his eyesight, he could have chosen to become bitter and resentful. Instead, he allowed God to turn his tragedy into holy ground. When I first met Michael in the spring of 2024, I could not believe his attitude and positive outlook. Rather than blaming a former friend for ruining his life, Michael sees his suffering as a gift from God, because it brought him to his calling. Michael has worked hard adjusting to blindness. Although new to the blind community, he has excelled with Lighthouse, a program for blindness, and he has even learned Braille. Best of all, Michael is prepared to minister to others by sharing his story and his faith. Michael may have spent much time in the desert before God got his attention, but today, God is using him to expand His kingdom because he chose to hear God's voice and listen.

You, too, may be walking through struggling, feeling all alone, having fled out into the desert because of your shame or your fear. God is kind to teach us even in the wilderness, but He also invites us to come home. While suffering may not end, His presence is a balm and a fire so that we might be ablaze in Him, ready to serve for His glory.

Chapter 5

Hold the Line: The Battle Is the Lord's

Can you imagine growing up in a world where there is little to no singing? This is how those people of the Chol tribe of Mexico lived until they encountered the gospel. In his book *Psalms of the Heart*,[14] author George Sweeting describes how two missionaries, sent from the Moody Bible Institute in 1947, traveled by both mule and canoe to reach a remote tribe located in southern Mexico. When missionaries John and Elaine Beekman arrived, they knew there was work to do, because there was no portion of the Bible available in the tribe's native language, let alone any pastors or churches to teach the people.

For twenty-five years, faithful missionaries labored to that end. After some time, the Bible was translated into the tribe's language. Soon after, there emerged a thriving church of over twelve thousand believers. One of the transformational results of the gospel upon the Chol culture was that they began to sing. The believers in the tribe became worshipers because when the gospel changes a heart, it comes forth from the lips: "He put a new song in my mouth, a song of praise to our God. Many will see and fear, and put their trust in the Lord" (Ps. 40:3).

Have you ever wondered what God thinks of singing? According to Scripture, He loves it. He not only enjoys when we sing to Him, but He sings over us: "The LORD your God is in your midst, a mighty one who will save; he will rejoice over you with gladness; he will quiet you by his love; he will exult over you with loud singing" (Zeph. 3:17). One reason God wants us to sing is because it is a way of sharing with others the good things He has done: "Sing to him, sing praises to him; tell of all his wondrous works!" (Ps. 105:2).

Some years ago, I was training pastors in Zanzibar, a small island off the east coast of Africa. The island is dominated by Islam. Ninety-nine percent of the population is Muslim, and the persecution against Christians is fierce. Yet, Muslims are coming to Christ. When I asked one of the local pastors what draws Muslims to Christianity, he smiled and said, "Our singing." He explained how Muslims are attracted to songs of Christianity because they are filled with hope.

Singing is designed by God. It is remarkable how the Lord can use it. Worship is a weapon in your own spiritual battles and a medicine for the suffering soul. As we will see, it was through the power of singing that God delivered His people and brought a great victory.

Insurmountable Odds

Jehoshaphat became king of Judah at age thirty-five. He had a heart to do what was right in the eyes of God because he had watched the spiritual failures of his father, King Asa. His father's example had shown that it matters more how you finish than how you start. King Asa had a great sensitivity to the Lord until later in his life, when he refused to rely on God (2 Chron. 16:7). Jehoshaphat would not make that same mistake.

Early in his kingship, Jehoshaphat faced an unprecedented battle. Three nations formed a coalition and planned to invade Judah. Judah could defend itself against one nation, but the threat of three would be insurmountable. So large was this unified army that the Scriptures do not ascribe a number to its size. It simply refers to the army as a "great multitude" (NKJV) and "great horde" (20:12).

While we may not be fighting physical armies, as Christians, we are engaged in a different kind of war. We fight spiritual battles. Our enemies may not be the Moabites or the Ammonites, but instead a highly sophisticated and organized "kingdom of darkness" (Col. 1:13 NLT).

Paul describes the kingdom of darkness in this way: "For we do not wrestle against flesh and blood, but against the rulers, against the authorities, against the cosmic powers over this present darkness, against the spiritual forces of evil in the heavenly places" (Eph. 6:12). In the original Greek language, Paul describes this kingdom using military language, suggesting an organized hierarchy. The point is that Satan knows what he is doing, and the threat of spiritual warfare was real then and is real today. Satan is always looking to oppose God's people. This is why he fights us so aggressively.

In this chapter, we will see how we daily encounter an Enemy just as lethal as the army King Jehoshaphat faced. Satan comes to steal, kill, and destroy (John 10:10), yet we are not defenseless, for God's promise remains: "No weapon formed against you will succeed" (Isa. 54:17 CSB). Together, let's discover how the battle is the Lord's!

When You Don't Know What to Do

King Jehoshaphat's first battle was with fear. When the report came that Judah was about to be invaded, he was "afraid" (2 Chron. 20:3). It is interesting that the Holy Spirit shows how this was Jehoshaphat's first reaction. Perhaps as you read this chapter, there are odds stacked against you, and you can see no way out. Defeat seems all but certain. Although King Jehoshaphat was afraid, Scripture tells us that he took his fear to the Lord and modeled for us the right way to pray.

Today, we can be tempted to pray small-minded prayers to an even smaller God. King Jehoshaphat's prayer was completely the opposite, because he saw God as sovereign and bigger than the problem: "Are you not God in heaven? You rule over all the kingdoms of the nations" (v. 6). The king's prayer teaches us that when we have the right perspective of God, then we will be able to put life's problems into the proper perspective. It is not possible to stand on God's promises while dwelling on negative thoughts or on what seems like a hopeless situation. One will crowd out the other.

Do you know why worrying is dangerous? Worry not only robs us of God's peace and steals our focus, but it also causes us to doubt His goodness. Worry has a way of pulling our mind and heart in multiple directions. The Greek word for "worry" is made up of two words: *merizo*, meaning "to divide," and *nous*, which means "mind." Consequently, worry means a divided mind. It should not surprise us when James wrote that "a double-minded man [is] unstable in all his ways" (James 1:8). Rather than feeling unspiritual when you experience fear and other negative emotions, you should realize that these are quite normal. You should step into the biblical invitation, "casting all your anxieties on him, because he cares for you" (1 Pet. 5:7).

Let's see how King Jehoshaphat handled his fear. According to 2 Chronicles 20:3–4, "Then Jehoshaphat was afraid and set his face to seek the LORD, and proclaimed a fast throughout all Judah. And Judah assembled to seek help from the LORD; from all the cities of Judah they came to seek the LORD." It is notable that the king went directly to the Lord before he solicited politicians, generals, and any other military leaders. Where do you go when trouble comes? Do you first look to the Lord?

When I was a young pastor, I encountered a situation that I did not know how to handle. I can remember taking my cell phone and calling people who I knew would pray for me. After making several phone calls, I sat tapping my phone, asking the question: "Who could I call next?" In a kind and gracious way, I felt the Lord say to my heart, "What about Me? You have called so many to pray for you, but you have not first called upon Me." What a wonderful lesson the Lord taught me that day. I do not need to first seek other people's advice. I need to seek the Lord.

My mind went back to my childhood pastor, who would often call Jeremiah 33:3 as God's telephone number:[15] "Call to me and I will answer you, and will tell you great and hidden things that you have not known." To this end, Amy Carmichael, missionary to India, once said, "Our loving Lord is not just present, but nearer than the thought can imagine—so near that a whisper can reach Him."[16] This is what King Jehoshaphat found to be true, and we, too, can experience it.

When Jehoshaphat was overwhelmed by insurmountable odds, he looked no other place but to the Lord: "If disaster comes upon us, the sword, judgment, or pestilence, or famine, we will stand before this house and before you—for your name is in this house—and cry out to you in our affliction, and you will hear and save" (2 Chron. 20:9). This is a wonderful Scripture to pray in times of trouble.

After reminding God of His promises and faithfulness, Jehoshaphat then prays one of my favorite prayers in the Bible: "We do not know what to do, but our eyes are on you" (v. 12b). If you are out of options and no one can help you, make Jehoshaphat's prayer your prayer.

A Strange Strategy

Planting a church is one of the hardest things I have ever done. Our first twelve months brought in a whopping twelve thousand dollars. The discouragement was crushing at times. The opportunity came to lease a new building, but the owner wanted two thousand dollars per month. Our fledgling congregation could not afford that large of a payment. However, we got creative, and the owner accepted a tax write-off deal.

Each month, we paid one thousand dollars and gave him a one-thousand-dollar tax write-off. Even with the steep discount, we had to believe God for every penny.

At this time, we did not have any other financial backing, so the only person to turn to was God Himself. At that point, I was only twenty-two years old. I did not need large donors. What I needed was more faith. I did not need church consultants. I needed God's strategy for growing His church. I remember moving my desk into the wide, spacious office that I knew deep down in my gut we were struggling to afford. It was not an extravagant office, but one thousand dollars per month might as well have been ten thousand.

In a hallway next to my new office was a small cubbyhole. I could feel the Holy Spirit telling me to place our monthly bills in this odd location. When God has shared strategies with me throughout the years, they are usually very detailed. I believe this is because God was teaching me obedience. God uses our obedience to bring His miracles, and obedience is in the details. The Lord was specific in His instructions. Not only was I to place the bills in the cubby, but I was to handwrite the chart of bills. As I look back at my twenty-two-year-old self, I see why the instructions were specific. God was teaching me the importance of giving attention to detail. He was teaching me the discipline of daily and weekly rhythms and the importance of obedience. God ensured that every one of our bills was paid each month. We sought Him in prayer, and He sustained us. While this is not a deliverance from a battle with sin, it was a very real provision that brought rest to the battle for anxiety about these bills in my mind. Sometimes we seek to find our best strategy, when really, we just need to turn to the Lord and ask.

As Judah sought help from the Lord, God was eager to answer. He said to them, "Do not be afraid and do not be dismayed at this great horde, for the battle is not yours but God's" (2 Chron. 20:15). When the Enemy attacks us, God takes personal interest. After all, it is His name and reputation on the line. Rather than giving our energy to fighting the battle, our energy should go toward trusting God. You may be on the battlefield, but rest assured, the victory is already won.

We often overlook God's answer because it can seem too simple. The people of Judah could trust that the battle was the Lord's: "'You will not need to fight in this battle. Stand firm, hold your position, and see the salvation of the Lord on your behalf, O Judah and Jerusalem.' Do not be afraid and do not be dismayed. Tomorrow go out against them, and the Lord will be with you" (v. 17).

When I first lost eyesight, there were times when I felt completely overwhelmed. Like King Jehoshaphat, I didn't know what to do. It seemed like nobody could help me, and there was no solution to be found. It was here that God taught me these Scriptures, and in my deepest moments of darkness, doubts, and confusion, the Holy Spirit would say to my heart, "Stand firm, hold the line, and see the salvation of the Lord." These Scriptures are not just what I teach, I live and breathe them.

Do you find yourself standing firm and trusting God, or does it seem you are doing all the fighting? It seems we are always in a struggle, and there isn't anything more exhausting than fighting your own doubts and vulnerabilities. Yet God has not called us to fight, because the battle is not ours—it is His. We are called to trust by standing firm in God's sovereignty. Thus, Paul writes: "Therefore take up the whole armor of God, that you may be able to withstand in the evil day, and having done all, to stand firm" (Eph. 6:13).

The Weapon of Worship

I was enjoying the enthusiastic worship as I visited a church deep in the mountains of Nicaragua, when my translator sat down beside me. "Do you see that pastor and his wife? You won't believe what happened to them this week." On this trip, we had traveled from town to town, training pastors and church leaders. I remember how one church was so remote that we had to drive our Jeep through a river to reach them. There was no electricity, and the only outhouse came with a warning to watch for snakes before using it. There was no parking lot, but rather hitching posts for horses, and sure enough, these pastors had traveled on horseback.

Pointing out this pastor and his wife, my translator continued: "Their house where they lived with their young daughter partially collapsed this week." While he told me this, I noticed both the pastor and his wife had their hands lifted. They were pouring out their hearts and worshiping the Lord, even though they were engaged in a fierce battle. I paid close attention to them through the rest of the service. From the outside looking in, you would never be able to tell that anything was wrong. They had warm smiles and what seemed to be an unshakable faith. Although they had no solution to their problem, they stood firm and held the line with worship.

The strategy for Jehoshaphat's battle plan seemed too simple: stand firm, hold the line, and see the salvation of the Lord. Rather than going into battle with mighty warriors, Jehoshaphat appointed singers and placed them on the front lines ahead of the army. Quite literally, they led with worship. How would you like to be in the choir on that day? Whether we know it or not, worship is a mighty weapon in spiritual warfare. We must remember that "the weapons of our warfare are not of the flesh, but are powerful through God for the demolition of strongholds" (2 Cor. 10:4 CSB).

What is leading the way when you are overwhelmed and facing insurmountable odds? Are you led by your emotions? Do the opinions of friends influence your decisions, or do you find yourself relying on your own judgment? Rather than looking inward, it is always better to trust in God's plan. Practically, this means engaging in genuine and authentic worship. The word *worship* comes from the Old English word *worthship*. It carries the idea of value. It literally means to give something of worth: our time, attention, energy, and affections. Worship is when you treasure God as your most valuable priority.

It is worth noting that the singers dressed themselves in "holy attire" (2 Chron. 20:21). Scripture encourages us to put on "the garment of praise" as our holy attire (Isa. 61:3). It is easy to walk around in negativity or have a critical spirit. If we are not careful, we will clothe ourselves with discouragement and despair. Instead, we must trade those garments of heaviness for garments of praise.

Worship is one of our strongest weapons of spiritual warfare because God inhabits the praises of His people. It is our praise that releases God's power to intervene in our circumstances. When the Nicaraguan pastor and his wife chose to worship during their calamity, they proved their trust in God's sovereignty, placing worship at the forefront of the battle instead of succumbing to worry or immediately planning to rebuild their home. And God, who promises to provide all our needs, was about to do just that. I asked my translator to find out the cost of repairing their home. I then shared their needs with friends who joined us in providing funds to rebuild what Satan tried to destroy.

Ambushed

God promised Judah that He was going to fight on their behalf. If they were obedient, they would see the salvation of the Lord. It is amazing to see the variety of ways God delivers His people. He used the mighty waters of the Red Sea to destroy Pharaoh and the Egyptian army. He used torches and pitchers to defeat the Midianites. He used the supernatural noise of chariots and horses of an angelic army to destroy the Syrians. For me, however, the most fascinating of all is 2 Chronicles 20:22—"And when they began to sing and praise, the LORD set an ambush against the men of Ammon, Moab, and Mount Seir, who had come against Judah, so that they were routed."

Judah was outnumbered three-to-one. Realistically, they were no match for this army, but on the other hand, this army was no match for the Lord of Hosts, the God of Battle. Neither is the kingdom of darkness any match for the God we serve: "What then shall we say to these things? If God is for us, who can be against us?" (Rom. 8:31). Do you feel that God, who lives in you, is stronger than the forces of darkness that oppose you? You can be confident that God is stronger, because we have all assurance that "he who is in you is greater than he who is in the world" (1 John 4:4).

When Judah presented itself for battle, it must have been something to see. One could not see soldiers on the front lines, but singers. Worship erupted on the battlefield and God intervened, confusing the various armies. The enemies turned on one another, and Judah did not have to fight, for the Lord fought for them (2 Chron. 20:23).

When thinking about obedience in worship and the power it releases, my thoughts return to a story I heard about a church overseas. A lady who was known by the church leadership to be faithful and trustworthy approached the pastor before the Sunday-morning service began. She shared with him how God told her to do a cartwheel across the stage. This woman was not known to be eccentric or sensational. In fact, she was quiet and reserved. I can only imagine what would go through my mind if someone in my church made the same request. Yet this pastor prayed and sensed that her request was from the Lord.

After the singing had concluded, the pastor announced to the congregation that something odd was about to take place, but that they were trusting the Lord for the outcome. She tucked in her shirt and did cartwheels across the stage. Suddenly, a man cried out from the balcony that he needed God. He ran to the altar and gave his life to the Lord that morning. To everyone's amazement, he shared how he came to church that day telling God that if He was real, have someone do cartwheels in the church this morning.

God is a deliverer! He had set an ambush for Judah's enemy that day. A man who was ensnared by Satan and enslaved to sin was set free by the power of the gospel (2 Tim. 2:26; Rom. 6:17). If someone asked me if cartwheels were an act of worship, I would probably laugh and answer a resounding, "No!" Yet on that day, because of this woman's obedience to the Holy Spirit, an ambush was released that set the man's soul free from the grasp of the Enemy.

God Will Turn It Around

God can turn our fiercest trials into our greatest blessings. When the people of Judah saw their enemies destroyed, they plundered the enemy by taking all their "goods, clothing, and precious things" (2 Chron. 20:25). As a matter of fact, there was so much spoil that it took three days to collect it all. On the fourth day, the people gathered in the "Valley of Blessing" because the people "praised and thanked the LORD there" (v. 26 NLT). What would happen if this became your new perspective? What battles could be won if praise and thanksgiving became your mentality?

The renaming of the valley is my favorite part of this passage. You and I must learn to do the same with our battles. By faith, what appears to be a valley of defeat can be a valley of blessing. The promise still stands: "When they walk through the Valley of Weeping, it will become a place of refreshing springs. The autumn rains will clothe it with blessings" (Ps. 84:6 NLT). The tears wept now will become pools of refreshing later. When we learn how to turn worry into worship, we will not surrender ground already won by Christ.

The result of this victory is that Judah "rejoice[d] over their enemies" (2 Chron. 20:27). The coming invasion they dreaded the most had turned to joy. That should encourage you in knowing that God can take what you currently dread and turn it for good that brings joy. When you grasp that truth, it will not be long before you find yourself rejoicing over the Enemy's loss.

Do you remember how earlier in the passage King Jehoshaphat was afraid (v. 3)? Do you recall how the Lord twice commanded Judah not to be afraid nor dismayed (vv. 15, 17)? All along, God knew His plans and the outcome. The same is true for us. This is the reason for the command: "Be strong and courageous. Do not be frightened, and do not be dismayed" (Josh. 1:9).

It is amazing how God reversed things. The fear that God's people once experienced was replaced with peace because God has not given us a spirit of fear (2 Tim. 1:7). Instead, the fear of God fell upon their enemies, and King Jehoshaphat and the people of Judah lived in peace (2 Chron. 20:29–30). The Lord fought for them while they worshiped.

Are you trusting God with your battles? "Some trust in chariots and some in horses, but we trust in the name of the LORD our God" (Ps. 20:7).

Chapter 6

Delays Are Not Denials: How to Wait on God

The uneasy woman sat across from me in my counseling office. She shared with me the struggles she was having as a young believer. Exhausted, she asked, "Do you think God can fix me?" I pondered her question saying, "Fix? You say that as though there is something wrong with you. Perhaps a better word is *complete*. Can God complete you and make you whole? He absolutely can!" In that moment, I felt hope fill the room.

Many of us are left worried that we might not be "fixable" and that we might have missed God's good plan for our life, and yet, that plan is simply this: "that you may be perfect and complete, lacking in nothing" (James 1:4). The word *perfect* can be translated "mature" (CSB). God's aim is that you be spiritually mature and emotionally whole. Is this not our goal as parents? Do we not desire that our children grow into mature, responsible adults? So this is the aim of our heavenly Father. The problem is that it does not happen overnight.

On my most difficult days, I try to remind myself that God's will is leading me toward a place of maturity—completeness—where I lack nothing. The Message translates "lacking in nothing" to "not deficient in any way." What a beautiful picture of God's desire for us. At the time of this writing, my youngest son, John Mark, is six years old. He recently asked me, "Dad, is being blind fun?" It was fascinating to me how his six-year-old mind was trying to process my blindness. "It's fun being your dad, and it's fun the way God uses my life and story," I said with a smile. While blindness is not pleasant, God has made my life enjoyable—full and lacking nothing in Christ.

Just as God is leading me, so He is leading you toward wholeness. The problem is that it is often a slow process. This is where most people stumble. Hardly anyone likes to wait, yet this is the way God has chosen to do His best work in us. There is a phrase tucked into James 1:4 that has changed my perspective: "Let steadfastness have its full effect . . ." The word *steadfastness* can also be translated "endurance" (HSCB), "perseverance" (NIV), or "patience" (KJV). Nevertheless, the word that thrills me the most is *let*. This reminds me that my responsibility is to trust God to do what He deems best. I need to allow Him to do His great work. The wise Christian will understand that it takes time to "let steadfastness have its full effect." In other words, there are no shortcuts. There are no quick fixes. Let the process play out.

Motivational speaker Les Brown often talks about the process of planting a Chinese bamboo tree. The plant takes a great deal of time of watering and nourishing without any payoff at first. After the first year, there is no evidence of growth. As the plant continues to be nurtured for the next few years, it still shows no signs of growth. However, in the fifth year, the bamboo grows a staggering ninety feet in only five weeks.

Brown asks the question: "Did it take five years or five weeks for the tree to grow?"[17] The obvious answer is that it took five years. Like the growth of bamboo, if we gauge God's activity in our life by only what we see, then we miss the bigger picture. God in His wisdom understands the strength of the root system required to sustain a ninety-foot tree. The waiting may be long, but the return is worth it. Too often we fail to understand that it takes time to grow roots in the Lord. Do you have the patience to wait on God as He nurtures your roots?

Amazon Prime Christians

Waiting on God is one of the most difficult experiences we go through. None of us likes to wait, especially in our age. Waiting can seem frustrating, discouraging, and even exhausting. However, from God's perspective, waiting can be the key that brings us sustained grace and strength and prepares us for His greatest work yet to come. Too often, we view waiting as an inconvenience, whereas God sees it as an opportunity to work in our lives. God has taught me how to wait, and I am thankful for it. My aim in this chapter is to help shape our perspective to see from God's vantage point. There is a blessing that awaits those who choose to trust God despite what their circumstances tell them.

It is important to remember that God always answers prayers. He may not give the answer we like or desire, but assuredly, He does answer. God will respond in one of three ways. At times, He will say, "Yes." He is a good Father, and according to James 1:17, every good thing in our life comes "from above." When we see God as good, and acknowledge the countless blessings and provisions He brings, this can lead us to gratitude and thanksgiving. Rather than simply enjoying the good things in our life, our enjoyment should result in worship. We can enjoy God by enjoying the good blessings He gives. In this way, His blessings are not an end to themselves, but a means for us to enjoy God.

Like a wise Father, there are other times God will say, "No." As a parent, it would be harmful to my children for me to say yes to everything they asked. The shortest route to raising future juvenile delinquents is to give kids everything they want. The wise parent will say yes often but also have the discernment to say no. There are times in my own prayer life that I think I am asking God for bread, but God knows it to be a stone. I may think I am asking for fish, but God knows it to be a serpent (Matt. 7:9–11). So, like a loving Father, in His wisdom, He will simply say no. We need to learn how to be as thankful for the times He says no as the times He says yes.

The third response is perhaps the most difficult. Often, God says, "Wait." It does not help that we are an Amazon Prime generation. Far too many of us expect our prayers to be answered the next day, as though God has a membership we can join. The reality is God doesn't work that way. Before losing eyesight, I could hardly wait at a red light, and I loathed sitting in waiting rooms. Today, I am amazed at the lessons God has taught me about waiting, and I hope to teach them to you.

As blindness settled in, so did patience. When I was forced to stop driving and lost mobility, it felt like my life came to a grinding halt. I can remember vividly those early days of sitting, waiting for someone to pick me up, to catch my next ride. I often felt overcome with frustration, but it was in those moments that the Holy Spirit taught me how to enjoy the fruits He was producing (Gal. 5:22–23). With my mind's eye, I would picture the fruit of patience and the sweeter the fruit became, the less frustration I felt.

Yes, God has taught me how to wait, and I am most thankful for it. From our perspective, waiting can seem frustrating, discouraging, and even exhausting. However, from God's perspective, waiting can be the key that brings us sustained grace and strength and prepares us for His greatest work yet to come.

God's Unsearchable Ways

Isaiah 40 is written for those who have but little strength. Isaiah's target audience includes the people of Judah and Jerusalem before the exile, during a time of major upheaval. They were waiting on peace, but instead would soon receive judgment due to their rebellion against God. They would soon again be waiting, this time in exile, hoping for a time that they would get to return. Waiting is often the hardest part of obedience, and God's people were not immune from this need. Isaiah 40:27 begins with the people of God complaining about Him: "Why do you say, O Jacob, and speak, O Israel, 'My way is hidden from the LORD, and my right is disregarded by my God'?" Now, these are not pagans who are far from God, but His children. Note how His children felt and the accusations they made. They are saying that God has abandoned them in their waiting and struggle, which they assume means He must also no longer care.

Many people know what it is to be bitter toward God. Ever been mad, disappointed, or let down by Him? The Enemy loves nothing more than for us to believe the lie that God does not care for us. He will shift our eyes to the Joneses or over to the Smiths and wonder why God helps them but doesn't seem to help us. He loves nothing more than for you to scroll through social media and wish you had someone else's life. *Why is my way hidden from God? Why are my prayers unanswered? Why does God answer other people's prayers, but not ours?*

My dear reader, I know these feelings from personal experience. I have preached crusades in Pakistan where God has opened blinded eyes, yet I remain in darkness. I have prayed over people in whom tumors have vanished, yet God has not healed me. While I rejoice in other people's answered prayers, I have often wondered why my way seems hidden from God; why I must be the one who waits. It can be so discouraging, which is one of Satan's favorite weapons.

Isaiah exhorts us to take our eyes off our complaints and negative feelings and, instead, direct our eyes and thoughts to the power and greatness of God: "Have you not known? Have you not heard? The Lord is the everlasting God, the Creator of the ends of the earth. He does not faint or grow weary; his understanding is unsearchable" (v. 28). While we may wait, a thousand years is but a day, and a day a thousand years to God

(2 Pet. 3:8). His ways are higher than our own, and always better (Isa. 55:8–9).

The phrase "his understanding is unsearchable" (Isa. 40:28) can alleviate many frustrations. Part of walking by faith is being okay with what we don't understand. In pride and arrogance, we often feel like we must have God figured out. The realization hit me a long time ago that if I understood everything about life and everything about God, then I wouldn't need Him. Consequently, it is because we see through a glass dimly that we need to trust God (1 Cor. 13:12). This trust is shown by our response to life's uncertainties. The mature believer will trust God even when he can't see what God is doing or allowing. Your faith will deepen when you take every doubt and question and apply the phrase, "Your understanding is unsearchable."

Do you remember how Isaiah shifted our eyes away from ourselves with all our complaints and accusations and put them on God? He then directs our eyes back to humanity, emphasizing our frailty: "He gives power to the faint, and to him who has no might he increases strength. Even youths shall faint and be weary, and young men shall fall exhausted" (Isa. 40:29–30). In other words, Isaiah is saying it doesn't matter how strong you may think you are. At some point, you are going to run out of strength. Or perhaps you chide yourself for not being as strong as you think you should be. Maybe you feel you get overwhelmed too easily. Isn't it encouraging to know that none of us is as strong as we think we are? The point of Isaiah 40:30 is that in our humanity, we fall short.

Worth the Wait

Blindness has taught me that God is worth the wait. If God does not waste any of our experiences, whether joyful or painful, then it is not a waste of time to wait on the Lord. That is confirmed by the psalmist: “Lead me in your truth and teach me, for you are the God of my salvation; for you I wait all the day long” (Ps. 25:5). Prior to blindness, I would have interpreted this verse as David saying, “Come on, God. Hurry up! Come through any day now!” Today, I read it with a different perspective: “I wait for you ‘all the day long,’ because You are worth the wait.” In other words, it is my pleasure to wait upon the Lord.

Waiting on God is worth any delay because God is working in us through the process: “Therefore the Lord waits to be gracious to you, and therefore he exalts himself to show mercy to you. For the Lord is a God of justice; blessed are all those who wait for him” (Isa. 30:18). Do you link God’s waiting with His grace? Isaiah did. Furthermore, do you love His glory more than your comfort? I have had to ask myself these questions many times, and if God is exalted and His grace abounds in my blindness, then I say God is well worth waiting on.

Last, God waits so that He may show mercy toward us. Once again, link God’s waiting to His mercy in your life. It will alleviate many frustrations, because “blessed are all those who wait for him” (v. 18). Can you see why there is such value in waiting? Those who wait will find His grace, His glory, and His mercy.

God Is Never Late

Two of my favorite heroes of the faith are George and Mary Müller. George and Mary lived and ministered in Bristol, England, and became world-famous for their orphanages. Early in their marriage, they pastored a small, rural church. In those days, people paid their tithe by renting their family's pew in the church. Often, the wealthier a family was, the closer they sat to the front. When Müller and his wife announced that God had led them to open an orphanage, few people supported them. In fact, his congregation became so upset that many refused to "rent their pews" any longer. While the withholding of their tithes may have discouraged some, it catapulted the Müllers into living by faith. Throughout the years, God blessed the orphanage, and the Müllers' faith was strengthened into a righteous oak.

One morning, in the mid-1800s, the orphanage had run out of food, but George Müller wasn't out of faith. To the staff's surprise, he ordered all three hundred children to be dressed, cleaned, and brought to breakfast for the meal God would soon provide. His staff had assured him there was nothing to be offered because the kitchen was completely out of food. However, Müller was convinced that God would not fail the children. Can you imagine three hundred hungry kids sitting in front of empty plates? Nevertheless, his faith did not waver. Müller prayed and thanked God for the food they did not have.

Suddenly, there came a knock at the door. It was the local baker, who asked if the children could use fresh bread. God had awakened him at 2:00 a.m. and burdened him to bake for the orphanage. Excitedly, Müller told the children, "God has not only given us bread, but fresh bread." Suddenly, there was a second knock at the door. It was the local milkman. His cart had broken down in front of the orphanage. He told Müller the milk would spoil before he could get it repaired. "Could the children use some fresh milk?" They brought in ten cans of milk, just enough to provide for the entire orphanage.[18]

There is a distinct group of people that can be seen in Isaiah 40:31, and they are not elite Christians. They are average, ordinary people like you and me. Yet what distinguishes them is their willingness to wait on the Lord. Note how Isaiah says, "They." This is not a category every Christian will fit into. Not everyone is willing to give God the space to work as He pleases. There are many who will find solutions of their own if God does not work with their time frame. However, others will submit themselves under the mighty hand of God and patiently wait.

Several years into my journey with blindness, God showed me something very special in Isaiah 40:31. He revealed the source of much of my frustration and impatience, and graciously showed the peace I was forfeiting. Rather than waiting on God, I had been waiting for my prayers to bring about a good outcome. However, Isaiah did not say that we are to wait for miracles, for fulfilled promises, or for our desired results. Instead, we are instructed to wait on the Lord.

Please do not misunderstand me. I believe God performs miracles in our lives today. However, the Lord showed me that I was growing in frustration because I was waiting for answers to prayer. Instead, God wanted me to learn to wait for *Him*.

And it is in the waiting that we discover the pleasures of God: "You make known to me the path of life; in your presence there is fullness of joy; at your right hand are pleasures forevermore" (Ps. 16:11).

Should you find yourself in God's waiting room today, consider if you are waiting for answers to prayer or waiting on the Lord Himself. Learning to wait on the Lord means becoming okay with the process, and praying, "Lord, work in me, 'both to will and to work for [Your] good pleasure'" (Phil. 2:13). When you settle in your heart that God is not going to be late, you can then enjoy learning to wait.

There is an adage that says, "Don't just enjoy the destination, enjoy the journey!" God wants you to enjoy your faith journey. Enjoy the different experiences that stretch your capacity, deepen your confidence, and strengthen your resolve to trust God. Enjoy the spiritual maturity that comes with every twist and turn of the Christian walk. You are on the adventure of a lifetime with an opportunity to uniquely glorify God by patiently waiting on Him.

Biblical waiting is not idleness. It is not sitting and allowing time to pass. The word picture in Isaiah 40:31 is that of serving. This idea is where we get our English word *waiter* or *waitress*—those who serve tables. This provides a different perspective of waiting on God. Therefore, we are to be serving while we are waiting.

Faith That Won't Waver

"They who wait for the Lord shall renew their strength" (Isa. 40:31). Notice the important word *shall.* This is significant because it is a promise, not a suggestion. If you are going to successfully wait on God, then you must take Him at His Word and stand firm upon His promises. No one did this better than Abraham, who had but one promise from God, yet we have been given thousands of promises in the Bible to stand upon. If Abraham could trust God for one promise, what can we do with thousands of them?

When God made a promise to Abraham, it took twenty-five years to come to fruition. Abraham was seventy-five years old when God told him he would have a son and be the father of many nations. Isaac was not born until Abraham was one hundred years old. The author of Hebrews chose Abraham as an example of faith. He instructs us to imitate "those who through faith and patience inherit the promises" (Heb. 6:12).

I have a world of appreciation for the word *imitate* because of the season of life I'm in. At the time of this writing, my two boys, Hudson and John Mark, are eight and six. I often laugh and call them Pete and Repeat, because John Mark does everything his older brother does. But isn't this the way we learn? We imitate by learning from those who are older, wiser, more mature, and farther ahead than we are. So it is spiritually. We should admire and look up to those who are ahead of us spiritually. That is why we are to "remember [our] leaders, those who spoke to [us] the word of God. Consider the outcome of their way of life, and imitate their faith" (13:7).

The apostle Paul pulls back the curtain to show us how to imitate Abraham's faith:

> As it is written, "I have made you the father of many nations"—in the presence of the God in whom he believed, who gives life to the dead and calls into existence the things that do not exist. In hope he believed against hope, that he should become the father of many nations, as he had been told, "So shall your offspring be." He did not weaken in faith when he considered his own body, which was as good as dead (since he was about a hundred years old), or when he considered the barrenness of Sarah's womb. No unbelief made him waver concerning the promise of God, but he grew strong in his faith as he gave glory to God, fully convinced that God was able to do what he had promised. (Rom. 4:17–21)

Twenty-five years is a long time to wait for a promise from God, yet these verses say there was no unbelief to cause Abraham to waver. The longer we wait, the louder unbelief can become. What was the key to Abraham's faith? He was "in the presence of the God in whom he believed" (v. 17). Being in the presence of God is the best place for learning how to patiently wait. If the only time you are in God's presence is occasionally at church, then you are missing the blessings of walking with God daily. In my own life, I do not face the day until I have first spent time in the presence of God. Do you have a daily time with God? Do you make it a priority to pursue His presence? "Without faith it is impossible to please him, for whoever would draw near to God must believe that he exists and that he rewards those who seek him" (Heb. 11:6).

Romans 4:18 further reinforces Abraham's faith by saying, "In hope he believed against hope, that he should become the father of many nations, as he had been told, 'So shall your offspring be.'" As each year passed, Abraham and Sarah's ability to bear children diminished. Yet, it did not sway his hope. People who don't understand faith will often say they don't want to get their hopes up, but faith is deeply related to hope: "Now faith is the assurance of things hoped for, the conviction of things not seen" (Heb. 11:1).

Even though his situation seemed hopeless, Abraham grew stronger in faith, not weaker. Can we really imitate such faith? The biblical answer is a resounding, "Yes!" Verse 20 holds the key to how we can grow in faith even during long seasons of waiting. It says that Abraham "gave glory to God." This principle will change your perspective during those times of waiting.

Some of my most difficult moments of blindness are when I go to my kids' ball games. Most days, I am content and highly productive. However, as my kids get older and they begin to play sports, I never feel blindness as strong as wanting to see them play ball. It is in these times that I feel the Lord asking me, "Chad, do you love My glory more than your comforts and your desires?" Although it is hard, I choose God's glory. I have found it to be a source of strength when I ask why or doubt God's goodness.

Glorifying God is such a central theme to the believer's life that Paul said we are to do it in everyday, ordinary tasks: "So, whether you eat or drink, or whatever you do, do all to the glory of God" (1 Cor. 10:31). Nothing glorifies God more than choosing to wait for Him during difficult times. If ordinary, daily routines like eating and drinking can glorify God, how much more do our sufferings? Only suffering gives us the unique opportunity to be patient as we wait for God to fulfill His promises.

Last, Paul said that Abraham was "fully convinced that God was able to do what he had promised" (Rom. 4:21). We gain this confidence by staying in God's presence (v. 17), by keeping our hope up (v. 18), and by giving glory to God (v. 20). These actions will cause us to be fully convinced of God's ability to do what He has promised in His Word and to find our strength only in Him.

Renewing Your Strength

Eagles have remarkable strength. They can fly at altitudes of ten thousand feet with speeds of thirty to forty miles per hour. At full strength, they have been clocked at speeds of one hundred miles per hour. Their vision is eight times that of a human, and their wingspan can reach up to seven feet. Their grip strength is a crushing four hundred pounds per square inch, ten times that of a human. This makes it more astounding that God compares our potential strength with eagles.

Eagles go through a molting process. This can be a dangerous time because it often leads to death. There are various reasons that can trigger the molting process: change in environment, infection, age, injury, improper nutrition, hormones, and genetics. I have to believe Isaiah had this in mind when he penned: "But they who wait for the LORD shall renew their strength; they shall mount up with wings like eagles; they shall run and not be weary; they shall walk and not faint" (Isa. 40:31).

When eagles begin the molting process, they become so weak, they lose the ability to fly. This bird, once capable of outflying any predator or storm, is now resigned to living in the valley. While in these valleys, eagles lose their feathers and become unrecognizable. As calcium builds up on their beaks, they lose their appetite and cannot eat. Many eagles die in this state, as it is only with the help of other birds that they receive food and avoid predation.

Perhaps you find yourself in a valley, unable to fly on the promises of God. You have lost your appetite for spiritual nourishment. The person you are today may seem unrecognizable to who you once were. Take heart, child of God. There is a promise for you, and it is that you shall renew your strength. You are not going to stay in this valley experience. There is fresh strength for you from heaven.

Be assured that Satan intends to steal your strength. He loves nothing more than for Christians to be isolated in dark valleys. Often, when he targets a believer's strength, he goes directly for their joy. This is why your joy cannot be found in the outcomes you are praying and believing for. Rather, joy must be centered in God alone. When He becomes your joy, then you will know and believe that "the joy of the LORD is your strength" (Neh. 8:10). This joy can be yours because it is not sourced from you. It is a gift given by Jesus. Isn't it extraordinary that joy does not come from ourselves, our circumstances, or even the outcome of our prayers? "These things I have spoken to you, that my joy may be in you, and that your joy may be full" (John 15:11).

When you understand that joy comes from Jesus, you can look beyond yourself or any pain or heartache and receive the joy Jesus wants to give you. This is why James 1:2 commands us to "count it all joy." Note how James does not tell us to feel joyful, but to choose joy. It is not a question of how you feel, but what you choose. The Greek word for "count" literally means to calculate or to evaluate. When you consider your present hurts or your past heartaches, you can take the joy Jesus offers and count these experiences as joy. The result of this will be strength.

Soaring Out of the Valley

Can you picture the once-majestic eagle, isolated and restrained to the valley? The only way the eagle survives molting is when healthier eagles come to its aid. Those who have overcome the valley know what it is like to be stuck there. Amazingly, these older, seasoned eagles hunt on behalf of the molting eagle living in the valley. As the weakened eagle begins to eat, fresh strength comes. The anemic eagle can then make its way to rocks, where it will beat the calcium buildup off its beak. The more it eats, the stronger it becomes. Soon it can soar out of the valley.

Perhaps you know someone currently in a valley. Similar to a molting eagle, they are weak and nearly unrecognizable. Don't give up on them. You have fresh meat that can strengthen them. You can pray and intercede for them. You can send them

Scripture and encouragement. These are the things that will bring them spiritual strength.

If you are the one in a valley yourself, take heart, because you are not defeated. The purpose of this book is to drop the fresh meat of God's Word to you, because I've been there, and I know the valley experience. Isaiah 40:31 is fresh meat for you whom God wants to see fly like an eagle. If you choose to accept it, your strength will be renewed. You will mount up with wings like the eagles. You will run and not be weary, walk and not faint. In other words, you're going to soar out of the valley!

Chapter 7

Risky Faith: But If Not

His influence was immeasurable, and Rome knew it. He was not only one of the strongest voices for Christianity during the second century, but he had been personally discipled by the apostle John. Now at the age of eighty-six, the Roman authorities were planning his demise. But God had already prepared the elderly bishop for things to come when He gave him a dream that his pillow was on fire. Polycarp discerned from the dream that Rome would burn him at the stake, because the city leaders hated him for refusing to worship their many gods and burn incense to the emperor.

On March 12, AD 155, the Roman authorities sent a squadron of soldiers to arrest Polycarp at his home. He neither ran nor resisted. Instead, he requested that he be given one hour to pray. How could they say no to this old gentleman? While Polycarp was praying for strength for what lay ahead, he ordered his servants to feed the very soldiers who had come to arrest him. After their feast and after Polycarp had spent time in prayer, he was led to the city's arena.

The people were in an uproar when they heard Polycarp had been captured. He was forced to stand before the proconsul in the city's stadium, which filled quickly with a bloodthirsty crowd. There, the proconsul demanded that he, "Swear by the fortune of Caesar; repent, and say, 'Away with the Atheists,'" Polycarp unflinchingly responded, "Eighty-six years have I served Him, and He has done me no wrong. How can I blaspheme my King and my Savior?"

The proconsul threatened, "I have wild animals here. I will throw you to them if you do not repent." Polycarp responded, "Call them! It is unthinkable for me to repent from what is good to turn to what is evil. I will be glad, though, to be changed from evil to righteousness."

Enraged, the proconsul warned, "If you despise the animals, I will have you burned." Resolute in his faith, Polycarp said, "You threaten me with fire which burns for an hour, and is then extinguished, but you know nothing of the fire of the coming judgment and eternal punishment, reserved for the ungodly. Why are you waiting? Bring on whatever you want."[19]

The book of Daniel introduces a group of friends who also faced the hot flames of adversity. Referred to as "the three Hebrew children," they were also known as Shadrach, Meshach, and Abednego. Their biblical story is famous enough to be mentioned in the "Hall of Faith," the passage in Hebrews 11 that lists men and women who were committed in following God and showing their loyalty to the Lord. Scholars believe that the prophet Isaiah was so influenced by the account of Shadrach, Meshach, and Abednego that he wrote: "When you pass through the waters, I will be with you; and through the rivers, they shall not overwhelm you; *when you walk through fire you shall not be burned, and the flame shall not consume you*" (Isa. 43:2, emphasis mine).[20]

The late author and Bible teacher Leonard Ravenhill wrote: "God and fire are inseparable."[21] Hebrews 12:29 states that God is an all-consuming fire. As noted in chapter 3, there is a holy fire that burns within a believer (Matt. 3:11). However, there are also trial experiences that Scripture defines as fire (1 Pet. 4:12). One is from within. The other is from outside circumstances. While these are two separate flames, they both serve the same purpose. Whether it is holy fire within or fiery trials from without, they come to cleanse and purify a believer's life.

There are many lessons to be learned in this story, but the aim of this chapter is to explain why God sees fit to take us through the fire. I hope to remove the belief that God wants us to avoid painful experiences at all costs. As we walk through this incredible story together, allow it to do for you what God intended it to do for every generation of the church: to strengthen your faith and deepen your resolve.

A Madman Worshiped

Daniel 3 opens with a name that would have struck fear in the heart of any Hebrew—*King Nebuchadnezzar*—a narcissist, an egomaniac, and a madman. His kingdom, the Babylonian Empire, was the superpower of his day. He not only took the people of Israel captive, but he often went toe-to-toe with God, demanding that he be worshipped instead of the true God. All the while, the Lord had allowed the rise of King Nebuchadnezzar because of the rebellious people of Israel.

Israel had been a nation under the rule of King Saul, King David, and King Solomon. From there the kingdom split into two nations—Israel, consisting of ten tribes to the north, and Judah, having two tribes to the south. Jerusalem was controlled by Judah; therefore, they stayed truer to the laws of God than Israel, who went into captivity much sooner than Judah. However, captivity eventually came to the entire kingdom.

God used King Nebuchadnezzar to bring into captivity Israel's finest young men who had remarkable skill sets and were quick learners. Those young men were then required to complete a three-year program that reconditioned them to Babylonian life and culture so they could serve the king. This reshaping of their identity required that their Jewish names be changed to Babylonian names, thus Daniel became Belteshazzar, Hananiah became Shadrach, Mishael became Meshach, and Azariah became Abednego.

These four had resolved not to defile themselves with Babylonian customs and culture, despite the king's attempt to strip them of their identity. They refused the king's food and did not drink the king's wine, nor did they worship his gods. Surprisingly, when they were evaluated by the king, he found their skills and abilities ten times greater than anyone in the kingdom (Dan. 1:20).

After this, Daniel and his friends were promoted to high levels of authority in the Babylonian government: "Then the king gave Daniel high honors and many great gifts, and made him ruler over the whole province of Babylon and chief prefect over all the wise men of Babylon. Daniel made a request of the king, and he appointed Shadrach, Meshach, and Abednego over the affairs of the province of Babylon. But Daniel remained at the king's court" (Dan. 2:48–49).

After this, God gave Nebuchadnezzar a disturbing dream that he did not understand. He called for the wise men of Babylon to give the interpretation, but they failed. When Daniel found out, he asked to be presented before the king. Though he was confident that God would give him the interpretation, he first enlisted the prayers of Shadrach, Meshach, and Abednego, asking God to reveal the dream and its meaning to Daniel.

To ensure the interpretation was genuine, the king refused to tell his dream to anyone. Whoever gave the interpretation was required to tell the king *what* he had seen. The king was stunned when Daniel told the king that in his dream he had seen a statue with a head made of gold, a chest of silver, thighs of bronze, legs of iron, and feet mixed with iron and clay. He was even more amazed when Daniel told him the clear interpretation of its meaning and then said, "You are the head of gold" (v. 38).

King Nebuchadnezzar's great pride and narcissism drove him to create his image in gold for all in the kingdom to worship. It was ninety feet tall and nine feet wide, and was set on the plain of Dura, in the province of Babylon (3:1). Rather than Daniel's interpretation causing the king to repent, his pride demanded that the entire empire see his statue glistening in the sun. He then made a decree that when music was played, everyone throughout the kingdom would bow down and worship the image (vv. 4–7).

Idolatry Today

Idol worship as I often think of it was not something I had witnessed until my trip to Vietnam near the Cambodian border. My friend traveled with me to this communist nation to smuggle Bibles to believers who were part of an underground church network. While there, I visited the famous Cao Dai Temple that held an enormous idol. It greatly stunned and saddened me to see hundreds of people singing, bowing down, and praying to this image.

Idolatry is the worship of someone or something other than the one true God. This has been Satan's goal since his rebellious fall from heaven: "I will make myself like the Most High" (Isa. 14:14). Satan's greatest desire is to be worshiped as God. This was his strategy when tempting Christ: "And he said to him, 'All these [kingdoms] I will give you, if you will fall down and worship me'" (Matt. 4:9). We see a similar motivation in King Nebuchadnezzar's demand for worship.

Although idols are usually foreign to Western culture, do not think for a moment that our society is not overflowing with idolatry. In today's church, many view worship as simply music. While music is an element of worshiping God, it is not the extent of true worship. The apostle Paul identified true worship when he said, "I appeal to you therefore, brothers, by the mercies of God, to present your bodies as a living sacrifice, holy and acceptable to God, which is your spiritual worship" (Rom. 12:1).

True worship is living life on God's terms and not your own. It means presenting your life as a sacrifice to God. As noted in chapter 5, the word *worship* comes from an old English word meaning "worth" and "ship." This is important to know because we worship what we value. Most people today do not value what God says nor what He thinks, and this is why it is rare that God is worshiped rightly.

God takes seriously His command, "You shall have no other gods before me" (Exod. 20:3). Satan hates this command, and that is why a spiritual war raged in Nebuchadnezzar's day and it is the reason why that same war rages today. Satan desires to draw our attention and affections away from God, so that we will place them on things of this world, which is idolatry. It is the wise Christian who embraces this profound truth.

Conviction That Draws a Line

When people ask how I handled transitioning to blindness, I tell them about the Mariana snailfish. Most likely you will not find these fish in an aquarium, because they live twenty-two thousand feet underwater. When first discovered, scientists puzzled over how these small fish could withstand the pressure at that depth. They discovered that these fish have gaps in their skulls that help balance the internal pressure with the external pressure of the ocean. Furthermore, their bone structure is largely cartilage. God's unique design allows these fish to handle extreme pressure.

I can relate with these fish that live in complete darkness. Just as God designed these small fish to withstand great pressure, His Word equips us to handle the pressures of life: "Little children, you are from God and have overcome them, for he who is in you is greater than he who is in the world" (1 John 4:4).

Shadrach, Meshach, and Abednego were about to face enormous pressure. Accusations were being made against them to King Nebuchadnezzar: "These men, O king, pay no attention to you; they do not serve your gods or worship the golden image that you have set up" (Dan. 3:12). The king became enraged and commanded that Shadrach, Meshach, and Abednego be brought to him (v. 13).

Nebuchadnezzar asked the three men if the accusations against them were true. Before they could respond, he gave them an ultimatum. When they heard the "worship" music, they were to fall on their knees and worship the golden image. If they did, all would be forgiven. They would keep their high positions in the kingdom and go on to live comfortable lives. However, if they refused to bow and worship, they would be thrown immediately into a fiery furnace and burned alive.

The response of Shadrach, Meshach, and Abednego is among my favorites in all of Scripture. The three men bluntly responded: "O Nebuchadnezzar, we have no need to answer you in this matter" (v. 16). In other words, "We don't have to think about this. There is no need to sleep on it. The line of our conviction is already drawn." We can only wonder where Daniel was during the dedication of the golden image and the sentencing of the three Hebrew young men. Perhaps he had been sent out of the country on official business. Had Daniel been anywhere within the empire of Babylon, he most certainly would not have bowed down and blasphemed the God of Israel. His refusal would have resulted in his arrest along with the three Hebrew young men.

Their position of faith is a great lesson for today's believers to be men and women of conviction long before pressure comes. Remember, these men had already resolved not to defile themselves in Babylon. They had spent years refusing the king's food and wine, so bowing to a golden image was not in the realm of possibility. Would you have that same conviction?

Pastor and Bible teacher John MacArthur observed that Shadrach, Meshach, and Abednego could withstand the external pressures of Babylon because their internal conviction was to serve the Lord only.[22] Like the Mariana snailfish swimming in the depths of the ocean, Shadrach, Meshach, and Abednego were surrounded by a sea of idol worshippers, but God had equipped them to handle the pressure. And God has uniquely equipped each of us to handle any pressure this world tries to apply . . . if we believe and trust God.

Faith That Plays It Safe

Nebuchadnezzar challenged Shadrach, Meshach, and Abednego, saying that their God could not deliver them out of his hand. Their response was: "If this be so, our God whom we serve is able to deliver us from the burning fiery furnace, and he will deliver us out of your hand, O king" (v. 17). How wonderful it is to have a faith that is fully persuaded and unwaveringly strong, steadfast, and sturdy, like a righteous oak (Isa. 61:3). For God alone is sovereign and has all ability to rescue us.

Shortly after the procedure that tore the retina in my left eye, I experienced debilitating intense pressure and pain. A normal eye pressure should not exceed 20 mm Hg. Prior to the procedure, I registered between a pressure of 14–15 mm Hg. After the failed surgery, my eye pressure fluctuated between a staggering 53–56 mm Hg. However, I was resolute and determined that the Enemy would not have the upper hand.

I returned to the eye doctor who had performed the surgery, and his solution to the pain was to remove the eye and replace it with a prosthetic. I rejected this suggestion. My conviction was then and is now deeply grounded in God and His ability to heal and to restore my eyesight. This apparently annoyed the doctor, and as he approached the door to leave the room, he turned toward me with a final comment: "When the pain gets bad enough, come back to me, and I'll take it out."

I left his office discouraged and bewildered. There was nowhere and no one to turn to but the Lord. Alone in my car and stopped at a red light, tears began to pour as I cried out to the God of heaven. In that moment, I felt the Lord impress on my heart to attend a prayer meeting a friend was hosting, so on a muggy Friday night in August, I went to this meeting and asked the men there to intercede for me. For over an hour, they fervently prayed for me. To God's glory, that night was the last time I felt pain in my eyes. My faith, along with the help of others, allowed me to withstand Satan's pressures, but the fiery furnace was yet to come.

It is impossible for me to read, listen to, or preach Daniel 3:18 without being stopped in my tracks. These three words may be the most faith-filled words in the Bible: "But if not . . ." I know many Christians who talk and sing about the goodness and greatness of God. But when pressure comes, they are not able to handle it, because their faith is a feel-good faith. This was not the case with Shadrach, Meshach, and Abednego.

The three Hebrew men were fully convinced of God's ability to rescue them, but they were also equally aware of the possibility that He may not: ". . . be it known to you, O king, that we will not serve your gods or worship the golden image that you have set up" (v. 18). What can Satan do with a resolve like that? Is your faith this sturdy? Would you feel the same toward the Lord whether He answered your prayer or not? The faith of Shadrach, Meshach, and Abednego was not dependent *on what God would do* for them. Their faith was secure *in who God is* and nothing else.

Facing the Fiery Furnace

When King Nebuchadnezzar saw the resolve of Shadrach, Meshach, and Abednego, it infuriated him. He commanded the furnace to be heated seven times hotter. This is where my Western, American thinking stumbles. If you are anything like me, it is hard to understand why God doesn't rescue them at this point in the story. They had passed the test by standing firm in their convictions before the king. So, why would God allow them to be thrown into the fiery furnace?

Perhaps this is where your faith falters as well. You feel like you have lived right. You can look back and see multiple tests that you have passed with flying colors, so why hasn't God rescued you yet? Why have these prayers gone unanswered? If anything, I learn in the story of the three Hebrew children that God does not prevent His people from facing the fiery furnace. Shadrach, Meshach, and Abednego were filled with faith, so much so that they even told the king "But if not . . ." Yet, it was God's plan all along for these three young men to be led into the fiery furnace.

In his pride and arrogance, King Nebuchadnezzar thought he was the one heating the furnace seven times hotter. In reality, God was preparing the furnace all along. As Warren Wiersbe aptly observed: "When God puts His children into the furnace, He keeps His hand on the thermostat and His eye on the thermometer."[23] The truth that is hidden in verse 19 is that the three Hebrew young men were not victims of a madman's anger. God was going to cause them to become victors, because God was in control in every twist and turn of this story.

We can overcome a victim mentality when we remember that God is in control. It may be that other people have wronged us; taken advantage of us; or even abused, neglected, or walked out on us. As the heat of life's furnace increases, it may feel like Satan is in control, but the fact is, God is in ultimate control, and this means He has the final say in the outcome.

According to verses 20–22, the king orders his men to bind the three Hebrew young men and cast them into the fire. Scholars believe these strong men were most likely the king's personal bodyguards. Can you imagine how rough they were with Shadrach, Meshach, and Abednego? Can you imagine how painful it must have been as they seized them and began to bind them? In my mind's eye, I wonder how long it took to prepare the furnace to be heated seven times hotter than normal. I wonder how far it was from the king's court to the furnace. I wonder how many thoughts went through their minds after having been so confident in God's ability to rescue. Did they doubt at any point that God had lost His power? Personally, I do not think so. Even if we are searching for Plan B, God is still faithful to follow through on Plan A.

When they reached the door of the fiery furnace, the flames were so hot they killed the strong men who had bound them. Why do you suppose it did not kill the three Hebrew young men? It is because God's power was already upon them. So it is with you, my dear reader. What would kill others is not going to kill you. What others can't handle, you can. "God is faithful; he will not let you be tempted beyond what you can bear. But when you are tempted, he will also provide a way out so that you can endure it" (1 Cor. 10:13b NIV).

Nonetheless, the three Hebrew young men fell, bound hand and foot, into the furnace. I would love to know how many people in the king's court watched these men fall into the furnace. Everyone had to have thought this was the end of the story. Would it shock you to know that many are watching your life? No doubt some think it's the end of your story. They watch you pray and believe, they see you keep your faith strong, but they honestly do not believe your situation will ever improve or turn around. Well, just like the king's court was wrong, so are they. God has not caused the fire in your life, but He has allowed it. God is writing a story with your fiery experiences, and the narrative is about His faithfulness. Let's watch the story unfold for these three men.

The Hotter the Flame, the Sweeter the Fellowship

Bible teacher Henry Martyn, who lived in the late 1700s, once said, "It should be the business of every day to be prepared for your last day."[24] Shadrach, Meshach, and Abednego were most certainly prepared, yet God had other plans. Scholars believe this fiery furnace would've been a deep pit in the ground. Perhaps Nebuchadnezzar had a balcony that overlooked it. Either way, what the king saw "astonished" him (Dan. 3:24). He was astonished because he saw four men, unbound and unharmed, walking around in the midst of the flames.

There was no explanation or human reasoning for what the king saw with his own eyes. The Hebrew word *astonished* means to be amazed. It carries the idea of being horrified and frightened. Nebuchadnezzar was frozen with fear as God wiped the arrogant smirk off his face. He shouted to his servants, "Did we not cast three men bound into the fire? . . . I see four men unbound, walking in the midst of the fire, and they are not hurt; and the appearance of the fourth is like a son of the gods" (vv. 24–25).

Who is this fourth man? Many scholars believe it was the Lord Jesus Christ. When Christ appeared in the Old Testament prior to His incarnation it is referred to as a Christophany. There are numerous such appearances in the Old Testament.

Christ is with His people in the fire. He was with the three Hebrew men, and so He is with you. The promise stands: "I will never leave you nor forsake you" (Heb. 13:5). There is a supernatural protection that comes upon God's people, because His presence is with us.

Corrie ten Boom and her sister Betsie experienced God's presence and protection on many occasions while suffering the brutality of Ravensbrück, a women's concentration camp during the Holocaust. Holocaust survivor Elie Wiesel said that if you survive the test, you must tell the story. This is exactly what Corrie did. Corrie and Betsie's harrowing story is documented in the classic book *The Hiding Place.* The inspiration drawn from their suffering is more than can be expressed. Betsie, who eventually died in that brutal camp, had said, "There is no pit so deep, that God's love is not deeper still."[25] Christ never leaves His people, for He was certainly with Shadrach, Meshach, and Abednego; He was with Corrie and Betsie; and He is with you.

The unwavering faith of these men and women point to a great principle: the hotter the flame, the sweeter the fellowship. As King Nebuchadnezzar stood frozen in fear, Shadrach, Meshach, and Abednego experienced a warm fellowship with Christ that only fire could have brought.

Nebuchadnezzar and the leading officials of Babylon had been eyewitnesses to a supernatural event. He had gathered the satraps, the prefects, the governors, and the counselors for the dedication of the golden image. Instead, they witnessed that the fire had no power over the bodies of the three men. We learn that even the hair on their heads was not singed, their cloaks were not harmed, nor did the smell of fire cling to them (Dan. 3:2, 27). This alone was miraculous. Anyone who has suffered a house fire knows that it is impossible to get the smell of smoke out of clothing and anything else involved in the fire.

Despite all that occurred, Nebuchadnezzar refused to acknowledge the Lord as the one and only God. Rather, he called Him "the God of Shadrach, Meshach, and Abednego" (v. 28). John MacArthur observes that the king's failure to repent after witnessing such an astonishing miracle was because he worshiped multiple gods. Therefore, in his thinking, the god of the Hebrews was simply at the top of the pile of all other gods.[26]

King Nebuchadnezzar never learned his lesson, but we can glean much from this story. God does not want us to fear the fiery furnaces when they come. Although He does not cause them, He is ultimately in control. If you believe that God should have rescued you a long time ago and you do not understand why you are still in the fire, perhaps Christ is calling you to a sweeter fellowship with Him. It may be that He wants to reveal more of Himself not only to you, but to the lost who are watching you go through your suffering.

God had a special outcome already prepared for the three young men when they came out of the fire: "The king promoted Shadrach, Meshach, and Abednego in the province of Babylon" (v. 30). Friend, there is promotion on the other side of your painful experience! Whether our promotion is in this life or the life to come, you cannot reach your full potential without the problems God has allowed you to face. Take heart because God knows what He is doing in your life. Many people think of faith as a place of comfort, but the story of Shadrach, Meshach, and Abednego proves that faith is anything but comfortable. Faith involves risk.

Faith That Risks

God often calls believers to take the risk of standing firm in their faith in Him. Many Christians today refuse to deny Christ, sometimes resulting in martyrdom. The three Hebrew men took that risk when they declined to worship King Nebuchadnezzar or any foreign god.

Polycarp stood firm in his faith and quenched the power of fire after refusing to have his hands nailed to the stake. He said, "Leave me as I am, for He that gives me strength to endure the fire, will enable me not to struggle, without the help of your nails." In his final prayer he exclaimed, "I give you thanks that you count me worthy to be numbered among your martyrs, sharing the cup of Christ and the resurrection to eternal life, both of soul and body, through the immortality of the Holy Spirit. May I be received this day as an acceptable sacrifice, as you, the true God, have predestined, revealed to me, and now fulfilled."[27]

As the executioner lit the fire, the flames quickly blazed around Polycarp. Eyewitnesses said that the flames formed an arch around his body like sails of a ship. When the proconsul saw that the fire would not consume Polycarp, he ordered the executioner to stab him. An entire stadium witnessed the miraculous that day. The miracle was not in God preserving Polycarp from the fire, but in his willingness to hold fast to his faith. Jesus said,

"Truly, truly, I say to you, unless a grain of wheat falls into the earth and dies, it remains alone; but if it dies, it bears much fruit. Whoever loves his life loses it, and whoever hates his life in this world will keep it for eternal life" (John 12:24–25).

Most suffering does not lead to martyrdom, but it will lead to a fiery furnace that tests faith. Let us not succumb under the heat of the fiery furnace; let us instead go over in victory. "For this light momentary affliction is preparing for us an eternal weight of glory beyond all comparison, as we look not to the things that are seen but to the things that are unseen. For the things that are seen are transient, but the things that are unseen are eternal" (2 Cor. 4:17–18). Therefore, hold firm to a faith that is secure in Christ—willing to risk all.

Chapter 8

Embarrassed by Jesus

Although I stopped driving in November of 2018, I still had enough peripheral vision in my right eye that I could navigate inside restaurants and other public places. Yet even that rapidly diminished, and by February of 2019, I was nearly completely blind. Sadie could see how much I was struggling. Of course, she was feeling the weight of the pressure herself. She booked us a wonderful Valentine's Day dinner at the Carnegie Hotel in our region. The dinner was hosted by Energize Ministries, an outstanding ministry to pastors based in North Carolina. It was supposed to be a night when pastors and their wives could connect to other leaders and enjoy a lovely meal together.

The problem was that the less I could see, the more I withdrew. I found myself more and more wanting to be alone. When I was with others, I felt like merely a shell. It was challenging to adjust from seeing people's faces to only hearing their voices. I tried my best to enjoy the Valentine's dinner and the wonderful couples at our table, but as conversations echoed all around me, I felt alone in the room. I was fighting discouragement and depression with every step.

When the evening came to an end, I told Sadie that I was going to visit the restroom. Although I had tried to adapt with every twist and turn of vision loss, this would be the first time I truly felt panicked. I was in a spacious restroom of a prestigious hotel, and I realized I could not find my way out. I kept circling around between the walls and sinks, but no matter how hard I tried, I couldn't find the exit. It may not sound like a big deal, but there in that restroom, I was hit with the overwhelming realization that I had just lost my independence and mobility.

As of this writing, the CDC reports that 28.7 percent of adults in the United States have some type of disability, in which 5.5 percent is blindness. I am one of them. Perhaps you are too. Whether you suffer from a disability or not, we can all relate to a certain man found in the Gospels whom Jesus healed from his infirmity.

An Ordinary Day

Scripture does not tell us his name. It only identifies him as the man with the withered hand. His story can be found in Mark 3. It is often just as fascinating to notice what the Holy Spirit omits as it is to focus on the details in the story. When I get to heaven, I look forward to finding people like the man with the withered hand. Like an investigative journalist, I have many questions to ask. I wonder if he was born with this deformity, or if he suffered a tragic accident. If so, how long had he been in this condition? Had he heard about Jesus before this momentous day?

While there are so few details about him, I feel like I know him. I relate to him and so will you, because everyone has a withered hand of sorts. It may be an insecurity, perhaps it is a past trauma, or it could be a present hurt. Either way, we all have some kind of vulnerability we want to keep hidden.

I imagine him to be a routine person. As someone with a handicap, I value predictability. I imagine him waking up at the same time each morning, eating the same breakfast, and enjoying his coffee while reading *The Jerusalem Post.* I guarantee he knew exactly how long it would take to get from the front door of his house to the front door of the synagogue. I imagine the Sabbath day being his favorite routine of all.

Perhaps he was one of the most consistent attendees. You could find him there week after week. I bet he was one of the first to arrive so he could sit in his usual seat, but one of the first to leave, not because he was unfriendly but because he avoided crowds and questions. He would talk to you, but only if you initiated the conversation. I imagine that no one in the synagogue knew the real story of what happened to his hand, because he didn't like to talk about it.

Called Out of the Shadows

Rumors were swirling about Jesus. People either loved Him or hated Him. Many important people hated Him more because He was a threat to their power, but ordinary people, like the man with the withered hand, appreciated all the good He was doing. Word spread quickly how He touched lepers, and they were cleansed of the disease. One story was told about a paralyzed man who couldn't get to Jesus, so his friends tore open the roof of a house and lowered him down to Christ, and he was healed. It seemed as though no disease could withstand Him. This and other stories like it would have been circulating widely in the area at the time.

So when the man with the withered hand saw Jesus walk into his synagogue on this particular Sabbath day, I wonder what went through his mind. Did he consider whether Jesus would touch and heal him? As a disabled man, perhaps he didn't. I have a feeling that he was very unassuming, that he kept his head down and minded his own business. He never dreamed that on this ordinary Sabbath day his life was about to change.

Like this man with the withered hand, Caleb, who was fresh out of high school, would slip in and out of the back of the auditorium on Sundays, mostly unnoticed. He wore a black hoodie and kept his head down and covered. Many people tried to engage him, but he didn't talk to anyone. It was clear he was uncomfortable. Yet, he kept coming back, week after week. People kept trying to engage him, saying, "Hi, would you like to sit with our family?" or "Hey, would you like a cup of coffee?" But Caleb declined.

Like so many kids growing up in America today, Caleb had zero exposure to church, let alone Christ and His gospel. He was taken to church only twice in his entire life—once to a small Pentecostal church, and the other was to Preaching Christ Church when he was about eight years old. What drew him to walk back into the doors of my church all these years later must have been the Holy Spirit.

After a month or so of attending Sunday-morning services, still standing alone against that back wall and making our safety team uncomfortable, he started showing up for Tuesday-night prayer services. I had eyesight back then. I will never forget speaking one Tuesday night when I noticed movement from the back. Caleb came out of his comfort zone and walked forward to the platform where I stood. I will never forget the look on his face when he said, "I don't know what's happening to me. All I know is I need God." And with that, he collapsed onto the floor beneath the weight of his sin. I immediately began to pray over him, as many others also responded. It felt like a spiritual emergency room, and God's people sprang into action. We called on the name of the Lord as Caleb surrendered his life to Jesus that night. Just like Lydia on the riverbanks in the book of Acts, the Lord marvelously opened Caleb's heart to the gospel.

When Caleb stood up, he was a new man. The old had passed away and everything in his life had become new. Weeks later, he was baptized. As he grew and became discipled, he eventually went through our ordination process. Today, he is a mighty preacher and strong in his faith, but back then he was in the shadows like the man with the withered hand.

When we come to Mark 3:3, the unthinkable happens. Jesus calls our friend forward. This had to feel devastating. He did not want all eyes on him. He did not want people asking questions or seeing his deformity. Of everyone who was there, why would Jesus call him forward?

Help in Our Hurts

Most people do not want to expose their hurts. We like to keep them hidden. In those days, people wore long, flowing robes. I imagine he kept his deformed hand tucked deep inside his robe so people would not see or stare.

I doubt people noticed the man with the withered hand that day, but Jesus did. Mark puts us in the room when he writes: "And he said to the man with the withered hand, 'Come here'" (v. 3). It probably surprised the disciples. It certainly surprised the Pharisees. But no one was more shocked than the man with the withered hand. When Jesus called him to come forward, I believe it embarrassed him. Speaking as someone with a disability, the spotlight was probably the last thing he wanted. Again, I know a little about this. I can't tell you what it is to walk through a crowded restaurant knowing all eyes are on you, or when I feel people hold their breath as I get on or off an escalator. Sometimes I wish I could hide my disability, but most people notice my blindness.

We all have withered hands of sorts, even if they are not physical. For many, they are mental or emotional. Larry and his wife, Susan, attended my church for several years before I knew about his "withered hand" of insecurity and hurt. Larry retired from the post office and has served faithfully in many different roles at my church. I have always seen him as a strong Christ-follower, but I had never seen his "withered hand," until one day we were ministering to the homeless of our city. We had gathered with all of them to pray, and I could sense a strong moving of the

Holy Spirit. I began to sing the chorus, "Oh, the blood of Jesus! Oh, the blood of Jesus! It washes white as snow."[28] This is when I heard the most beautiful voice harmonizing, and I was stunned to find out it was Larry. After the service that night, I asked him how I never knew that he could sing.

Larry had been hurt several years prior at a previous church. Since then, Satan had isolated Larry and kept his gift of singing tucked away. We all have this same tendency. When we get hurt, we lean toward isolation. This is exactly what Satan wants us to do. Satan would have us tuck away our hurts, insecurities, and vulnerabilities. Lysa Terkeurst says it this way in her book, *It's Not Supposed to Be This Way*: "If Satan can isolate you, he can influence you."[29] Satan does his best work in the dark.

When I first went blind, a hundred different things embarrassed me. I remember walking through the lobby of my church and accidentally running into a lady who had her back turned to me. I was so embarrassed. During a prayer service, I was teaching on the main floor rather than the stage. Without realizing it, I had taken several small steps and had slowly drifted, no longer facing the congregation. Someone had to come forward and turn me around to put me back in the right position. I was mortified. I found it embarrassing when people tried to talk to me, but I couldn't make out their voice and I had to ask who it was. For me, the most exhausting part of it all was the embarrassment. So, I found myself wanting to tuck my withered hand away to where people couldn't see it.

I slowly became a recluse. As soon as I finished preaching, I would go back to my office where I didn't have to talk to people.

It wasn't because I was unfriendly. It was because I was embarrassed. In the beginning of blindness, I found it so difficult to be in public. When I was out to eat, I would inevitably spill my drink or food.

In those early days, the greatest difficulty was the emotional weight of my suffering. I did not know what to do with the trauma of going from a fully sighted husband and father to a completely blind man. To be honest, I didn't even know it was traumatic at the time. I simply dismissed it and pushed through. Looking back on it now, this was not God's will. It was not His will for me, and it is not His will for you. God cannot heal what we hide. God cannot help what we are not willing to expose.

Moved to Act

While the Pharisees sought to trap Jesus as they asked if it was lawful to heal on the Sabbath, Jesus was unrestricted by the extra rules they had placed around the Law and, instead, expressed the heart of the Law Giver: that people might be healed from the ravages of what sin has done to them. When Christ saw the hard hearts of the Pharisees and their willingness to ignore the needs of the people around them, it made Him angry (Mark 3:5) because they were not going about the Father's business: to see people given hope. This was righteous anger, anger toward injustice and wrongdoing.

The Pharisees hated Christ because He challenged their authority. He did not fit into their religious box, and they despised Him for it. Mark tells us the motive the Pharisees had when they came to the synagogue that day: "And they watched Jesus, to see whether he would heal him on the Sabbath, so that they might accuse him" (v. 2). Jesus had nothing good to say about the Pharisees. He made it clear that His mission was "to seek and to save the lost" (Luke 19:10).

There is a difference between righteous and sinful anger. When anger is rooted in sin, it creates space for the devil to work in our lives. We can be angry without sinning (Eph. 4:26), but sinful anger invites the devil into our situations. Thus, Paul writes: "Give [no] place to the devil" (Eph. 4:27 KJV). The CSB calls it "opportunity," and the NIV calls it "foothold." The Greek word Paul used is *topon*. This is where we get our English word *topography*. When you react in sinful anger, you are surrendering ground to the devil. It is forfeiting and giving up ground already won by Christ.

In sharp contrast, a righteous anger is quite healthy. When Christ saw the Pharisees' hard hearts, His compassion shifted to the one that needed Him the most—the man with the withered hand. When people ask my advice on how to know what they are supposed to be doing for God, I start by asking, "What makes you angry?" In other words, what bothers you—even irritates you—and causes you to lose sleep is often where God is leading you. When you find what stirs passion within your heart and it is in line with the direction of God in His Word, that is how you know where you are called to serve.

My wife, Sadie, grew up in a nominal Christian home. Her family took her to church, where she learned the plan of salvation, and even responded to it, yet she was never discipled. Today, discipleship is her greatest passion. The thought of people checking religious boxes without fully following Christ stirs in her a righteous anger, which leads her to action—to discipling others and sharing the truth of the gospel. This righteous anger leads her to move.

Is there a righteous anger in your life? When you see homeless people, does it make you say to yourself, *Someone should do something about this?* or are you moved to be that "someone"? When you think of children trapped in the foster care system, does it bring a righteous anger to your heart, knowing that someone should adopt them? Perhaps that is God's call for your life. Find what makes you righteously angry and seek to serve. God might use you to relieve the suffering of another, just as Jesus did as He ministered to the man with the withered hand.

Stretch It Forth

After Christ challenged the Pharisees, He turned His attention back to the man with the withered hand. I can see this disabled man standing in front of all these people. Perhaps he could feel the judgment of the Pharisees quickly giving way as he felt compassion from Jesus. There is much we can apply to this Gospel account.

When Jesus called him forward, he could have refused and stayed seated, or worse, ran for the exit, but he didn't. Instead, he obeyed. Without knowing what Jesus would do or what others would say, he obeyed the command. It was this simple obedience that led to a miracle. As if the man was not embarrassed enough, Jesus really pushed him over the line when he looked at him and said, "Stretch out your hand" (Mark 3:5). What hand? My deformed hand? My hand that I keep hidden so that other people do not ask questions? Stretch out my vulnerability, my insecurity? Here is the point: Miracles happen. When we do what we can (obedience), God will enable us to do what we can't.

I would've loved to have been in the room that day as the man stretched forth his hand. Before everyone's eyes, Jesus did a creative miracle, and the man's hand was restored. Wouldn't you have loved to have seen it? Had I been there that day, I would've shaken that miracle hand, or at least given him a high five!

The Sunday I preached this passage, I was surprised to find Larry waiting to see me. For the first time, he showed me his "withered hand." Through tears, he shared with me the hurt he had experienced in other churches. He told me how this had suppressed the gifts and callings on his life. But that morning, he was called out of the shadows. Larry declared, "Pastor Chad, from now on, I am going to stretch out my withered hand." Over time, God has healed those past hurts in Larry's life. When we shine God's light on what Satan has done in the dark, it changes everything.

Today, Larry is a leader in our church, and he often leads us in singing with his beautiful voice. Every time I hear him sing, I remember how he stretched out his "withered hand" and God restored it. Have you allowed past traumas or even present hurts to shape and define who you are today? Jesus would say to us, "Stop hiding it and stretch it forth." Jennifer Rothschild, who is a gifted Bible teacher and accomplished author, is also completely blind. I love how she puts it: "Blindness does not define me. It refines me!"[30] She has learned what it is to stretch it forth. How do you need to stretch out your withered hand today?

Chapter 9

A Holy Heist: Answered Prayers We Don't Believe

"Stop praying!" What an odd feeling to be halted by the Holy Spirit. Has God ever stopped you from praying? To say that I was feeling overwhelmed would be an understatement. I was still adjusting from the failed surgery that had torn my left retina, leaving me permanently blind in that eye. About the same time, I was feeling led to form the teaching ministry, Awakened to Grace.

As I worked to establish this new ministry, my eyesight was rapidly deteriorating in my right eye. In the early days of Awakened, our opportunities were small, but our funds felt even smaller. Like any endeavor for God, it took faith. With my first big contract almost due, I decided to host a fundraiser. The event was successful, but it left me twenty-five hundred dollars short. I can remember how hard I worked toward that fundraiser, and how disappointed I was to come up short. I did not say anything publicly about the twenty-five hundred. I simply asked God to provide it.

The following Saturday, I awoke early and began to pray fervently about this financial need. I prayed with all my might.

It was at this moment when the Holy Spirit directed me to stop praying. It was a most peculiar moment with the Lord. I realized I had been praying out of a sense of panic rather than with faith. I felt the Holy Spirit say to me, "Stop praying! Your prayers have been heard, and they have been answered." All of a sudden, an unusual peace came over me. I decided to rest in the promises of God and trust that they are "yes and amen" through Christ (see 2 Cor. 1:20).

Later that afternoon, I went to the church office. When sorting through the mail, I noticed an envelope addressed to me from another church in my city. To my complete surprise, it was a check for Awakened to Grace for twenty-five hundred dollars! I could not believe how specifically the Lord had answered my prayer because I hadn't even made the need publicly known. I then felt the Holy Spirit prompt me to notice the date of the check. It had been made out early in the week. The Lord showed me how I had spent all week praying with a sense of panic, whereas in all reality, the check had already been cut, sealed, and mailed. How many times does God answer prayers we don't believe?

This chapter is about God's ability to answer prayer and rescue His people. When the early church gathered for earnest prayer, the stakes were much higher than waiting for a mailed check. Many were facing life or death. While they experienced miracle after miracle, they still faced the potential danger of failing to believe God for the things they prayed for. And yet today, we are in the same danger of praying but not believing. As we will see, God responded to the church's prayers for Peter's release. He sent an angel to break Roman chains and to open iron gates.

Still today, God responds to the prayers of His people, but do we expect it? Like the early church, could our miracle be knocking at the door, but we don't believe?

Pressures Within, Persecutions Without

Acts 12:1 paints a vivid picture of the persecution that the early church was facing: "About that time Herod the king laid violent hands on some who belonged to the church." To understand the context of this persecution, we need to go back earlier in Acts. In Acts 4, we see that the church began to face persecution from without, with Peter and John being arrested, beaten, and threatened by authorities. In Acts 5, we see tensions begin to rise from within the church. This is seen in Ananias and Sapphira lying about a financial gift, costing them their lives.

Due to the rapid growth of the church, needs were beginning to distract the apostles from their mission. Widows were being overlooked, so the church began to establish deacons and other leaders. One of these deacons, Stephen, became the first martyr in Acts 7. By the time we arrive at Acts 8, persecution is widespread. In fact, Acts 8:1 mentions God scattering His people due to persecution. The word picture for this in Greek is an image of scattering seed. The gospel was about to spread throughout the known world as never before.

In Acts 11, the prophet Agabus predicts a worldwide famine, causing even more strain in the young church. We see the churches coming together at the end of Acts 11 to help one another.

The early church was under intense pressure from both without and within. But despite the persecution, the church continued to grow and spread the gospel. The early church is a powerful example of how God can use even the most difficult circumstances to accomplish His purposes.

The name Herod is mentioned throughout the Gospels and Acts. At first glance, this can seem confusing, since many "Herods" are found in Scripture. Herod was not one individual king but rather the name of several members of a dynasty that was appointed to govern Jewish Palestine under Roman rule. When Christ was born, Israel was ruled by Herod the Great (Matthew 2). When Christ began his earthly ministry, it was Herod the Great's son who ruled, Herod Antipas. He is the king who beheaded John the Baptist (Matthew 14). By the time we reach Acts 12, we find Herod Antipas's son, King Agrippa I. Finally, his son, King Agrippa II, judges Paul's case in Acts 25.

The Herod dynasty was hostile to Christianity. According to Luke, Herod Agrippa I killed James, the brother of the apostle John and one of the original twelve disciples of Christ (Acts 12:2). James was among Jesus's closest inner circle. He nicknamed James and John the "Sons of Thunder" (Mark 3:17).

When Herod saw that the Jews were pleased James had been killed, he proceeded to also arrest Peter, a figurehead of the early church. Luke tells us that this takes place during "the days of Unleavened Bread" (Acts 12:3). These would be the days leading up to Passover. We can only imagine what a long and difficult week this would have been for the early church.

A Miracle Set in Motion

The early church was not only familiar with persecution by the authorities, but they were also marked by prayer. It was through earnest prayer that God enabled them to withstand times of persecution. It is interesting to me that when Luke says the government "laid violent hands" on the Christians (v. 1), they did not organize political rallies or protests. There was no petition campaign. Instead, the church gathered for prayer.

Peter had been imprisoned for a week, with Herod about to execute him. He finds himself sleeping between two soldiers and bound with two chains, with soldiers guarding the prison doors. This is the third time that Peter has been imprisoned, and Herod was taking no chances. He put four squads of soldiers around Peter, sixteen men in total, and he chained Peter to two soldiers. It seemed like there was no way for Peter to escape. In the middle of the night, an angel of the Lord appeared and released Peter from his chains. The angel led Peter out of the prison and past the sleeping guards. Peter then escaped to safety (vv. 6–11).

This is a miraculous story of God's deliverance. It shows that even when things seem hopeless, God is still in control. He can deliver us from any situation, no matter how difficult it may seem. Peter's escape from prison is a reminder that God is always with us, even when we are in difficult circumstances. He is always willing to help us, if we ask Him.

Resting in the Lord

Stunningly, Luke tells us that on the night of Peter's execution, he is sleeping (v. 6). Do you suppose you could sleep, knowing that the next morning you would be killed? Do you know why Peter and the other disciples did not fear death? After Christ rose from the dead, He appeared to His disciples on many occasions. In Mark 16, the angel sent word to His followers, including Peter, that Jesus was going before them to Galilee. There they would see Him, just as He had told them (vv. 6–7). Peter and the disciples saw, touched, and worshiped the risen Lord Jesus. This is why they never feared death again.

Perhaps Peter remembered the words of Jesus in John 21:18, that he would not die until he was an old man. Yes, he would give his life for the cause of Christ, but it would not come until years later. Whether it was this promise or knowing that the church was praying earnestly, either way Peter was able to slip off into a deep sleep under the most intense circumstances imaginable.

Do you find yourself resting in God's promises? Most of us are not facing circumstances as dire as Peter, yet so many of us have been robbed of peace, joy, and many good nights of sleep. We should learn from Peter's example of what it means to rest in the promises of God.

I will never forget the Saturday night before I preached this text. I spent two years preaching through the book of Acts. All the while, I was rapidly going blind. I was already completely blind in my left eye, and I was experiencing the same breakdown in my right. Late Saturday night, after my family had gone to bed, I was in my home office putting the finishing touches on the next morning's sermon. All of a sudden, a blood vessel burst behind my right eye. All I could see was a thick, dark streak. I panicked as I felt my shirt instantly drench with sweat. I fell to my knees and pleaded with God to not take my eyesight. It was not a prayer of faith, but of dismayed fear.

I will never forget how the Holy Spirit quieted me. A holy hush settle over my panicked state. I could sense the Lord telling me that if Peter could sleep the night of his execution, I, too, could go to sleep and rest confidently in the sovereignty of God. I dried my tears, stood up, and went to sleep reminding myself that God is sovereign and God is good. I slept like a baby that night.

I don't know about you, but Peter's story convicts me. Peter's problems were much more dire than mine, and yet, he was able to rest in the Lord. Am I able to rest in the Lord? You and I know there are some sins we just don't think are that big of a deal. Worry is often one of these. "Well, it's just how I am," I've had people tell me. "Well, my mother was a worrier, and I'm just like her." "I can't help it. It's just how I'm wired. It's just who I am." On the contrary, as a new creation in Christ, worry no longer has a hold on you. You've been set free from its clutches. You and I need to take that seriously.

When you and I worry about the circumstances of life, what does this tell the Lord? It tells the Lord, *I have to deal with this. I have to take control. I have to carry it.* We're saying, *God, you don't have the power to help me.* Andrew Murray, missionary to South Africa, said it so well in the 1800s. He said, "God is much like our bed. In Him, we can lie down and rest."[31] Are you resting in the Lord today? Are you resting in His promises? Are you resting in His sovereignty, in His wisdom? Are you resting in His ability to help you?

So the next time you can't sleep because you're worried, your mind is fretting, or you're feeling overwhelmed, go to Acts 12 and tell the Lord, *If Peter could sleep in the prison, I'm going give You what's going on in my life. You God, You'll take care of it. I am weary, and I know that You give me rest.* Do you know that sleeping is sometimes one of the most spiritual things you can do? Do you know that sleeping can be worshipful? If you go to bed and ask God to handle the situation that is keeping you awake, this is worship. It's worship to say, *God, I'm not worrying about it anymore.* We worship God when we humble ourselves, admitting we're not strong enough, powerful enough, mighty enough, or even wise enough.

An Angel Dispatched

Do you believe angels are active today? Scripture teaches they are. Just as an angel came to the aid of Peter, so God sends them to help us as well. The promise still stands: "The angel of the Lord encamps around those who fear him, and delivers them" (Ps. 34:7). I do not think it is strange nor unusual for angels to be involved in our daily activities.

The author of Hebrews helps shape the way we should think and feel about angels. We are to never worship or even pray to an angel. Hebrews 1 confirms Christ's superiority over the angels. In fact, He is the Creator of angels and is worshiped by them (Heb. 1:6; Luke 2:14). When the apostle John, feeling overwhelmed by the sights and sounds of heaven, fell down to worship the angel who was guiding him, the angel replied, "You must not do that! I am a fellow servant with you and your brothers the prophets, and with those who keep the words of this book. Worship God" (Rev. 22:9). Why are we to not worship angels? It is because they are not God, and only He is worthy of worship.

While angels are not God, they are assigned by Him: "Are they not all ministering spirits sent out to serve for the sake of those who are to inherit salvation?" (Heb. 1:14). According to this verse, angels are sent to serve us. It is remarkable to think that we, once lost in darkness and now redeemed and forgiven by God, are served by His holy angels.

Bible expositor A. W. Pink gives a fitting example of this in his day. He observes that when Queen Elizabeth II was born in 1926, she had many attendants serving her needs. Each of her servants was older, wiser, and stronger than her, yet they served her.[32] What was the difference? She was royalty. So it is with us. Although angels are eternal, holy, and far wiser and stronger than us, we are the sons and daughters of God. We are a "chosen race, a royal priesthood, a holy nation, a people for his own possession, that you may proclaim the excellencies of him who called you out of darkness into his marvelous light" (1 Pet. 2:9).

So, on the night of Peter's execution, while the church is gathered, praying fervently for God to intervene, an angel is dispatched to Peter's cell. Luke sparks our imaginations, putting us right in Peter's cell: "And behold, an angel of the Lord stood next to him, and a light shone in the cell. He struck Peter on the side and woke him, saying, 'Get up quickly.' And the chains fell off his hands" (Acts 12:7). Can you picture this angel arriving on the scene and filling the cell with the light of God's glory? Perhaps he did not expect to find Peter sound asleep. I find this verse nearly comical. Luke says the angel had to strike Peter on the side just to wake him up. Friends, that is a deep and restful sleep!

The Chains Fell Off

While Peter is sleeping and the church is praying earnestly, God is working, and a miracle is set in motion. However, the problem in the natural realm was that Peter was still chained to Roman guards. While it is great that the angel arrived in the cell, he did not possess the key. So it is with our difficulties. So often we can see the spiritual side but still dwell on the natural side. We may believe in prayer, yet at the end of the day, many of us are still bound with thick, heavy chains.

Chains are heavy and weigh us down. Perhaps you have felt in your own life the tension between things of the Spirit and natural limitations beyond your control. The beauty I see in this text is that when prayer sets miracles in motion, God orchestrates every detail. Peter not having keys was not a problem for God. Note how the text says, "the chains fell off." No key was needed. So it is in our difficulties. God is not limited by what limits us. God takes the natural and supersedes it with the supernatural.

God can do through prayer what cannot be done in the natural. You may think your spouse is never going to come to the Lord, but God can break the chains of unbelief in an instant. You may think your prodigal children are too far gone, yet God can break their chains of rebellion. Perhaps you feel you will never be free of addiction, but God's miracles are boundless and know no limits. Just as God awakened Peter, he can awaken our loved ones. Just as God set Peter free, He can set you free.

The Right Response

God was faithful to answer the prayers of the saints. He dispatched the angel to Peter's cell. He put the guards into a deep sleep, and He supernaturally broke the chains. Now it was time for Peter to do his part. After commanding him to get up quickly, the angel said, "'Dress yourself and put on your sandals.' And he did so. And he said to him, 'Wrap your cloak around you and follow me'" (v. 8).

While the prayers of the saints had the miracle in motion, Peter could have missed the outcome had he continued to lay there. Imagine if he wanted to sleep for another few hours or expected the angel to come back at sunrise. What I love about the way God works is that it involves both God's part and our part. Yes, God may be answering many of your prayers right now, but it will still require obedience from you. We must respond rightly to God's interventions.

Warren Wiersbe helps us understand these Scriptures with a simple yet profound insight. He observed what an ordinary daily task it is to clothe ourselves and put shoes on. Part of our obedience may be in the simple and routine moments of your life. Don't miss God in these moments. Wiersbe noted that Peter most likely never dressed himself and put his shoes on again that he did not think of this incident in King Herod's prison cell.[33]

As Peter and the angel slipped past the Roman guards, they came to the outside gate. Luke tells us that an iron gate led into the city. This would have likely been a strong and sturdy fortification for the city. Yet, just as the angel broke the chains, so he could open the gate. Luke then says the gate "opened for them of its own accord" (v. 10). John Piper does well in reminding us that gates do not have an accord.[34] They do not have decision-making abilities. What does this say to us?

If we know that we're praying to a God who can open gates, if we know we're praying to a God who can rescue Peter out of his prison, if we know we're praying to a God who can break open chains, and if we know we're praying to a God that can put Roman soldiers to sleep, then why do we pray so little? Prayer changes everything. John Phillips, that great British expositor, reminds us that when King Herod's iron gates slammed shut, heaven's gates flung open as God's people prayed.[35]

Where to Go When Trouble Comes

After accomplishing his assignment, the angel vanishes, leaving Peter alone in the streets of Jerusalem. According to verse 9, Peter thought this entire experience was a vision. Now, standing alone in the brisk night air, he is wide awake (v. 11) from the deep sleep we saw in verses 6–7. When the guards would soon wake up, they would realize Peter had escaped. Where was he to go?

Without GPS or Google Maps, he makes his way to Mary's house. Mary is the mother of John Mark, who wrote the Gospel of Mark. Many scholars believe Mary's house is where Jesus and His disciples celebrated the Last Supper just before the crucifixion. Either way, Mary's house would have been considered a "safe house" for Christians in Jerusalem. We know from verse 12 that it was a large house that could accommodate many believers, because they had gathered for all-night prayer.

There is a lesson here for us. When Peter was in trouble, prayer meeting was the first place he chose to go. Where do you go when you are in trouble? As a pastor, it saddens me when I see people who are in trouble running away from God rather than toward Him. I once had a woman tell me she was too weighed down with the cares of life and too overwhelmed to make it to church. She thought church was the last place she needed to be, but in fact, it was the best place for her. I greatly appreciate how Peter ran toward this prayer meeting.

While God wants us to pray and worship in solitude, He has also designed His body to be together. There is a unique strength that comes when believers worship and pray together. So where will you go the next time everything falls apart? Run toward God's people, not away from them, because there is strength there for you.

Prison Gates and Prayer Gates

When was the last time you were shocked by God answering a prayer? Sometimes I think of the early church as perfect

Christians. It doesn't take long reading the book of Acts to see many of their imperfections, and I am thankful for this. In Acts 12, the church of Jerusalem had been gathered for prayer for seven days (the week of Unleavened Bread). James had been martyred, and many of their brothers and sisters had been thrown into prison by King Herod, who had "laid violent hands" on the church (v. 1). Knowing Peter would be executed at Passover, they continued in constant, earnest prayer. God answered their prayers by dispatching an angel and orchestrating one of the greatest heists in history. The problem is that, now the answer to their prayer stood knocking at the door, but they didn't believe it.

Luke says, "And when he knocked at the door of the gateway, a servant girl named Rhoda came to answer. Recognizing Peter's voice, in her joy she did not open the gate but ran in and reported that Peter was standing at the gate. They said to her, 'You are out of your mind.' But she kept insisting that it was so, and they kept saying, "It is his angel!" (vv. 13–15).

We can all learn from this story. Rhoda was completely convinced that Peter was at the gate, but the very ones who were praying didn't believe. How many Christians today argue with one another? Some say God still does miracles, while others say they have ceased. I, for one, do not want to be among those who try to explain the power of God away. I do not want to give time and energy to prayer, only to not believe that God is either unable or unwilling to answer prayer. It stuns me that these early Christians, who may have been present for the day of Pentecost, the healing of the lame man in Acts 3, and the house that shook under the power of God in the prayer meeting in Acts 4, were now unable to believe that their prayers were answered.

Are you a Christian who would rather argue about the things of God than engage and participate in them? This is a pretty good example of the church today, isn't it? As it turns out, Rhoda wasn't wrong. In fact, it was Peter, and Luke tells us that he continued knocking until someone came to the gate. Can you picture Peter, having just been miraculously rescued from prison, now stranded on the streets of Jerusalem? Think of the absurdity of the situation. The iron gate of the Roman prison opened of its own accord, but now the gate to the prayer meeting is locked tight. Yet here is another lesson for today's believer.

Don't get discouraged when you have to persistently keep knocking on a door. Peter could have easily said, "God, You helped me back there. Why won't You help me right now?" Why does it seem that God will answer some prayers but not others? Why is it that the prison gate opened but the prayer gate didn't?

Thankfully, Peter was persistent. When they did finally open the gate, they were amazed to see him. You can imagine their joyful shouts. Luke describes that Peter motioned with his hand to quiet them. After all, he was the most wanted man in Jerusalem now. Instead, Peter wanted them to share the story of his deliverance with James and the other brothers. He is speaking here of James, the leader of the Jerusalem church, the brother of Jesus.

There are many of you with a testimony like Peter. Your chains may not have been physical, but you know what it is to be bound with anger, lust, greed, or jealousy. God has rescued you out of bondage. Just as Peter wanted his story told, are you giving testimony to what has happened in you? Revelation 12:11 says Satan is overcome "by the blood of the Lamb and by the word of [our] testimony." How long has it been since you've told others what God has done for you?

Up to this point, the narrative of Acts has been primarily about the ministry of Peter, but after chapter 12, he fades from the storyline as Paul begins to emerge. The point is this: The very miracle they prayed for stood knocking at the door, but no one but Rhoda believed it. Perhaps your miracle will soon be knocking. Will you be looking for it? As your prayer life grows, so should your expectation of seeing God's miracles.

King Herod's Death

Peter was rescued. God was glorified. And King Herod was made a fool. In a rage, Herod had the soldiers who were supposed to be guarding Peter put to death. He then traveled to Tyre and Sidon, located in modern-day southern Lebanon. According to verse 21, the king put on his royal robes, took his seat on the throne, and delivered an oration to the crowd. They responded: "The voice of a god, and not of a man!" (v. 22). Luke says, "Immediately an angel of the Lord struck him down" (v. 23). Could this be the same "angel of the Lord" that rescued Peter from prison? I believe it is. King Herod, who so opposed the people of God, could not stop this gospel movement. After his death, "The word of God increased and multiplied" (v. 24).

This reminds me of another man in history who was hostile to Christianity. Yet, the anger he spewed toward God could not stop Christianity from advancing. Voltaire was a French philosopher of the Enlightenment who lived from 1694–1778. He is famously attributed with saying that one hundred years from his day, the only place you will be able to find a Bible is in museums.

Voltaire lived a godless life and died a tragic death. It is said that as he took his last breaths, he felt the flames of hell lapping at his feet. Like King Herod, Voltaire was wealthy but had no regard for the things of God. James 1:10–11 warns: "Like a flower of the grass he will pass away . . . the rich man fade[s] away in the midst of his pursuits."

Colonel Henri Tronchin, along with other European Christian businessmen, purchased Voltaire's estate after his death. They turned it into the largest Bible depot for all of Europe. Isn't that just like God? Just as the Word of God increased and multiplied in the book of Acts, it increased and multiplied throughout Europe, and it is increasing and multiplying in our day through the efforts of those who labor in Bible translation and distributing to various people groups. The promise still stands: "The grass withers, the flower fades, but the word of our God will stand forever" (Isa. 40:8).

Chapter 10

Shipwrecked: The Storm of Your Life

According to *Time* magazine, scientists predict that the twenty-first century will be known as the Century of Storms.[36] Who can forget Hurricane Katrina, that slammed into New Orleans in 2005; or Superstorm Sandy, that hit the northeast in 2012; or most recently, Hurricane Helene, which not only devastated the Gulf Coast, but also ripped five hundred miles inland through my home region of East Tennessee and Western North Carolina?

Storms are inevitable. Jesus taught that people either build their lives on a foundation of solid rock or on shifting sands. When the rain fell and the winds blew, only the house that was built on a firm foundation survived (Matt. 7:25–27). Jesus taught that when storms come, we are to be ready.

Not long ago, I went to a department store to purchase new clothes. Shopping was not enjoyable when I had eyesight, so imagine how much less I enjoy it as a blind man. Clothing stores are hard to navigate being blind, because they put displays and clothing racks in the middle of aisles. When I was greeted by the pleasant sales associate, she offered help to find the correct sizes and colors. After finding what I needed, she began to ring up my purchases and asked what I did for a living. When I told her I was a pastor, she said, "Hey! You're that blind pastor I've heard so much about."

I paid for the transaction and then, to my surprise, she moved from behind the counter and stood beside me. There was emotion in her voice when she quietly asked, "Will you pray for me?" Tears began to flow as she shared about her recent divorce and how she and her children were struggling through the greatest storm of their lives. Together we prayed, and suddenly the department store became holy ground.

Grace That Is Sufficient

Paul is often called the apostle of grace. His life is a demonstration of how the grace of God can bring someone out of darkness into light. Paul was not exaggerating when he called himself the chief of sinners (1 Tim. 1:15). But notice how Paul describes his newness of life: "But by the grace of God I am what I am, and his grace toward me was not in vain" (1 Cor. 15:10a).

Grace was such a central theme to Paul's writings that he seemed to use it as a unique fingerprint to prove the authenticity of his letters to the churches.[37] The first time we find grace mentioned in the Bible is in the story of Noah and the ark. Noah found grace in God's sight (Gen. 6:8). When Christ walked the earth, John described Him as being "full of grace and truth" (John 1:14). Yet no one articulates grace quite like Paul, because he experienced such deep and personal transformation. It not only turned him from a sinner to a saint, but it strengthened and sustained him through all his sufferings.

Paul faced numerous dangers and persecutions, many of them detailed in 2 Corinthians 11:24–26. Yet in contrast to these, he faced a particular suffering he called a "thorn in the flesh" (12:7). I have spent a great deal of time praying and thinking about what this thorn in the flesh could have been. I agree with most Bible teachers who conclude that Paul's physical suffering may have been his eyesight.

When he visited the Galatians, he came to them with a physical condition, yet they did not dismiss him or make fun of him: "You know it was because of a bodily ailment that I preached the gospel to you at first" (Gal. 4:13). Paul provides more insight on what this condition may have been when he wrote: "If possible, you would have gouged out your eyes and given them to me" (v. 15). Furthermore, when he penned his letter to the Galatians, he wrote it with "large letters" by his own hand, suggesting once again the condition of failing eyesight (6:11). Based on this evidence, my belief is that the thorn in Paul's side was vision loss.

Paul concluded that his sufferings prevented pride and conceit. This is often the case. I sometimes wonder how King Saul's story might have been different had God given him a thorn in the side. Likewise, in all of King Solomon's wisdom, he still fell to the blinding power of pride. Had these men and subsequent generations of people learned the valuable lessons Paul was trying to teach, then pitfalls and dangers could be avoided. Clearly, God is repelled by pride, but He is attracted to humility.

One of the most frustrating aspects of suffering is trying to make sense of it. But Paul grasped the "why" of his sufferings. In 2 Corinthians, he pulls back the curtain and allows us to see how God uses temporary sufferings to produce an eternal purpose. When we walk through seasons of suffering, we want and need answers, as did Paul. So, when he asked God to remove the thorn in his side, God's answer was, "My grace is sufficient for you" (12:9). For most of us, that is not the answer we want. And it is no different in my situation, because I would like God to change my condition. The reality is that God wants to change me.

Paul shows us step-by-step how this happens. First, Paul teaches that God's grace is sufficient. Grace that is sufficient means it lacks nothing and will never run out. One of Paul's favorite sayings was grace that abounds (Rom. 5:15–20; 2 Cor. 9:8). The Greek word for "abound" is *perisseuei*, which gives a word picture of a river that overflows its banks. This is why Paul says that where there are waves of sin, there are greater waves of grace (Rom. 5:20). Can you picture a perpetual river that never runs dry? This is the imagery of God's grace on our lives.

Second, when grace is activated and working in full measure, we experience the power of Christ at work. God continues by saying, "My power is made perfect in weakness" (2 Cor. 12:9). Satan's intent is for us to embrace our strengths or remain stuck in our weaknesses. Either way, we will stay inadequate and anemic in our faith. Yet God gives us a different perspective. He wants us to embrace our weaknesses, for those limitations always provide an opportunity for God to display His strength and power.

Charles Spurgeon had the right viewpoint of weakness when he wrote: "God does not need your strength: He has more than enough power of His own. He asks for your weakness: He has none of that Himself, and He is longing, therefore, to take your weakness, and use it as the instrument in His own mighty hand. Will you not yield your weakness to Him, and receive His strength?"[38] What does it mean for God's power to be perfected in our weakness? The idea of perfection is when God's power reaches its full potential. What a contrast to our limitations and weaknesses!

Someone once told me that life can either grind you down or polish you up. Paul had the latter perspective. He teaches that we should view sufferings with an eternal outlook. Satan would love nothing more than for you to grow bitter while you suffer. A man named Jake attended my church when we were both in our twenties. Jake had moved out of state, and I lost touch with him. Twenty years later, I ran into him when our ministry was feeding the homeless in our city. Now in our forties, we could not believe that twenty years had passed so quickly. Sadly, life had grinded him down in homelessness. Jake's curiosity prompted him to ask, "Chad, you have served God faithfully all this time. Why would He allow you to go blind? I know why I am homeless. It is because of the choices I have made. But you've been faithful to God. How is it that you're not bitter toward Him?"

Paul's words have guarded me from becoming resentful or bitter toward God: "For I consider that the sufferings of this present time are not worth comparing with the glory that is to be revealed to us" (Rom. 8:18). Note what he writes to the

Corinthian church: "For this *light* momentary affliction is preparing for us an eternal weight of glory beyond all comparison, as we look not to the things that are seen but to the things that are unseen. For the things that are seen are transient, but the things that are unseen are eternal" (2 Cor. 4:17–18, emphasis mine). It is interesting that Paul views his suffering as "light" when compared to the great glory that awaits him. Do you look at suffering through this lens? Are your expectations of the glory to come like that of Paul? If not, the rest of this chapter will help you gain this kind of perspective, because God takes the storms of life we experience and makes us better. You are not going to go under. You are going to go over, because, in Christ, we are conquerors (Rom. 8:37).

The Storm of Your Life

Paul had the rare and unique opportunity of being a citizen of both Israel and Rome (Acts 22:28). When he stood trial before King Agrippa II, he appealed to Caesar in Rome. It has been well said that while Paul dreamed of going to Rome as a preacher, God sent him there as a prisoner. Little did he know the way Satan would oppose him on his voyage. Paul would encounter the greatest storm of his life and suffer a devastating shipwreck, yet there are life-changing principles we can learn from the catastrophe Paul experienced on the Mediterranean Sea.

The ship headed to Rome had 276 passengers. This included the crew, the Roman soldiers, and the prisoners (27:37). Scholars have observed that the only way Paul's companions, Luke and

Aristarchus, could have accompanied Paul on this voyage was if they surrendered their personal freedom and became prisoners of Rome (v. 2). Luke, who authored the book of Acts, writes with such detail and precision that it makes the reader feel as though we are in the ship ourselves with the apostle.

When they reached the port at Fair Havens, most of the crew did not want to spend the winter there, so they decided to sail on. Julius, centurion of the Augustan Cohort, was convinced to continue their journey due to a south wind that was gently blowing (v. 13). The deception of the gentle wind convinced them it was safe to sail, despite Paul's warnings (vv. 10–11).

The storm these men encountered is known as a Euroclydon. This is a type of northeaster that occurs in the Mediterranean Sea with hurricane-force winds. The term *Euroclydon* is thought to be a combination of the Greek words *Eurus* (a southeast wind) and *Clydon* (meaning "wave" or "storm"). So severe was the storm that, according to verse 20, neither the sun nor stars could be seen for many days.

Both natural and spiritual storms are an inevitable part of life, attempting to blow us off course. We all encounter them, as did Jesus and the disciples on the Sea of Galilee. When a storm beset Jesus and His disciples as they crossed the Sea of Galilee, Jesus rebuked the wind and waves and the storm stopped (Mark 4:39). The Greek word for rebuked is *phimoo*, which means to silence, restrain, or put a muzzle on. This is the same word Jesus used when He cast out demons throughout the Gospels. In the same way He rebuked demons, He rebuked this storm because He has authority over all created things: both natural and spiritual. Storms come and toss us around, but there is hope because Jesus quiets them and directs our paths.

Through Many Dangers, Toils, and Snares

It was a horrific storm that began the internal conversion of John Newton.[39] Born on July 24, 1725, in London, England, Newton grew up during the height of the transatlantic slave trade. His mother, Elizabeth, knew the Lord and instilled Christian values in her son. Sadly, she died when John was only six years old. This loss and the lack of her godly influence would lead Newton down paths of sin and rebellion throughout his youth. However, the gospel seeds that his mother had sown in him would not lie dormant for long.

John was left to be raised by his father, who earned his living as a shipmaster. The rough seas were a tough environment for raising a son. It did not take long before the immorality and unrighteous living of his fellow sailors found their way into John's heart. John eventually served in the British navy and later became captain of his own slave ship.

In those days, families in Africa were ripped apart by those operating the slave trade industry. They were transported on slave ships in the most horrendous and unsanitary conditions. They were sent to England and America to be sold. It was through a fierce storm on the Atlantic, off the coast of Ireland, that God got the attention of John Newton. A veteran of the open seas, John was no stranger to storms, but this storm was different. It caused him to cry out to God. He promised the Lord that if his life was spared, he would become a changed man. While the change was not instantaneous, the process had begun.

As a pastor, I often see this process play out. In Christianity, we love to celebrate dramatic conversions, but we should also be intentional to celebrate the conversions that take a while. I love nothing more than to see a Saul instantaneously converted into a Paul, but I also love to see the doubting Thomases and the denying Peters walk out their faith and resolve their doubts and questions. John Newton did not immediately begin to follow Christ, but he opened his heart to the idea, and over the next few years, he would become soundly converted by the grace of God.

Newton knew that he needed to walk away from the evils of the slave trade industry, so he took a job as a tide surveyor in 1754. He then lived the next ten years in Liverpool, becoming established in his faith. During that time, he felt a draw toward ministry and eventually became a pastor in 1764. Newton served faithfully as a pastor for forty years. In 1772, God enabled Newton to write the world's most famous and beloved hymn, "Amazing Grace."

"Amazing Grace" deeply moves me when singing or hearing, "Amazing grace! How sweet the sound, that saved a wretch like me! I once was lost, but now am found; was blind, but now I see." Through that song, we can almost see John Newton crying out to God from that slave ship, knowing the brutality and wickedness of his lifestyle. Nonetheless, he experienced God's amazing grace.

In Newton's old age, he became a prominent figure in the abolitionist movement in England. He greatly impacted and influenced the life of William Wilberforce, a British politician whom God used to abolish slavery in the United Kingdom. As a little boy, Wilberforce grew up listening to Newton preach and was greatly influenced by his teaching, his moral stance on slavery, and his story.

The part of John Newton's life that resonates most with me was his blindness. In his old age, Newton lost eyesight, yet he remained faithful in shepherding the flock God had given him, opposing slavery and mentoring the next generation as with Wilberforce. Though blind and nearing the end of his life, he said, "My memory is nearly gone, but I remember two things: that I am a great sinner, and that Christ is a great Savior."[40]

Newton died on December 21, 1807, and was buried on the church grounds of St. Mary Woolnoth, where he had pastored for forty years. His tombstone reads: "John Newton, once an infidel and libertine, a servant of slaves in Africa, was, by the rich mercy of our Lord and Savior Jesus Christ, preserved, restored, pardoned, and appointed to preach the faith he had long labored to destroy."[41]

It was a great storm, the storm of his life, that led Newton to cry out to God and eventually receive eternal life. Newton's physical life ended in 1807, but at that moment, his eternal life began with the God whom he so faithfully served. When thinking of John Newton in heaven today, it is fitting to remember these words that he penned in 1772: "When we've been there ten thousand years, bright shining as the sun, we've no less days to sing God's praise than when we'd first begun."[42]

When Hope Seems Lost

Like John Newton's storm, the great storm Paul and all aboard the ship battled was fierce, lasting fourteen days. Imagine how exhausted they would have been after two weeks of constant hurricane-force winds. After the crew threw all they could overboard to lighten the ship, Luke writes: "all hope of our being saved was at last abandoned" (Acts 27:20). Like those on the boat, many of us find ourselves in circumstances where we have exhausted all options to change the conditions. Perhaps, you are in a tempest and feel as though all hope is lost. But be encouraged! It was at Paul's point of despair that God sent a messenger to him.

An angel appeared to Paul and gave him a specific word of hope: "Do not be afraid, Paul; you must stand before Caesar. And behold, God has granted you all those who sail with you" (v. 24). Notice that the angel told Paul not to fear. With this new encouragement, Paul said to the men, "I urge you to take heart, for there will be no loss of life among you, but only of the ship" (v. 22). He was able to give the men of the ship encouragement, because he had a word from God.

Friends, you have something far greater than an angel. You have the very words of God in Scripture. Take hold of God's promises. Hide them within your heart. Commit them to your memory, and you will not only find yourself being strengthened, but you will have the ability to strengthen and encourage others. Paul believed what the angel told him, and he spoke truth to the crew even when it seemed all hope was lost. What would change if you began to speak faith and victory in the middle of your storm? It is so easy to criticize and become negative. We should be careful to pay attention to what we are saying in the middle of hardships. Let us learn from Paul how to respond to fierce storms. Let's be in agreement with what God says and speak that truth to ourselves and others. Like Paul, you belong to God, and you worship God. This is why you are kept by God.

Christians are built for storms. Psalm 92:12 says the righteous will "flourish like the palm tree." Palm trees are extremely resilient in storms. God made them so unique that they can survive sustained winds up to 140 miles per hour. Like a palm tree, you might bend, but you won't break.

Palm trees can survive harsh conditions because of their unique root system. Unlike other trees, they do not have a taproot system. Instead, they have thousands of roots that enable them to survive the harshest of conditions, whether drought, heat, or hurricanes. Amazingly, palm trees are stronger in the aftermath of a storm than before. When a palm tree is bent under the force of wind, it strengthens its root system. As a palm tree can survive the fiercest storms, we can also survive the storms of life when we are rooted in Christ and established in our faith (Col. 2:7).

Sustained Through the Storm

In times of crisis, it is easy to overlook our spiritual well-being. The instructions Paul gives tell us what to do during our own times of difficulties. Paul did not withdraw when the

Roman soldiers and the crew ignored his warning not to set sail. It would have been easier to isolate himself and grow bitter. Instead, Paul reinserted himself and became the leader of the ship. Even Julius, the Roman centurion who was in charge, began to look to Paul for direction.

When we go through the storm of our life, we must be careful to not let Satan steal our influence. When we are hurt or ignored, it's so easy to withdraw and isolate, but just as the soldiers and crew needed the spiritual insights of Paul, so the people in your life need your spiritual insight.

Taking the lead, Paul urged the men to eat. They would need their strength, because God promised they would make it to shore. They would lose the ship, but they would not lose their lives. Paul was so sure of this promise that he used a biblical idiom, telling them that not one hair would perish from their heads (Acts 27:34). Christ had taught this in Matthew 10:30 and Luke 21:18. With that strong assurance, Paul then passed out food.

The lesson to be gained is that we cannot neglect spiritual nourishment, especially during a storm. It is in the chaos, violent winds, and uncertainty that we need God's Word the most. How easy it is to fall out of church, disconnect from small groups, and neglect our time with the Lord when life seems to pull the rug out from beneath us. Yet it is in those times of uncertainty that we need the clarity of God's promises the most. We should be running toward God and the things of God and not away from them.

You may ask, "What is spiritual nourishment and its importance?" One source of spiritual nourishment is the Word of God found in Scripture: "Your words were found, and I ate them, and your words became to me a joy and the delight of my heart" (Jer. 15:16a). Christ Himself is the "bread of life" (John 6:35). Spiritual maturity is when we grow from the milk of Scripture to the solid food of Scripture (Heb. 5:13–14). Nothing can replace the nutrients that Scripture gives to a growing believer, and if we are going to face storms, we'll need to do so with nourished strength.

Another source of spiritual nourishment is knowing and doing the will of God. Jesus told His disciples, "My food is to do the will of him who sent me and to accomplish his work" (John 4:34). Natural food sustains us by maintaining our health. It satisfies our hunger and strengthens our physical bodies. What natural foods do for the physical body, spiritual nourishment does for the soul. If you want to be healed, sustained, satisfied, and strengthened, discover and do God's will. Paul was in the direct will of God sailing to Rome, and although Satan tried to prevent the journey, he was able to receive nourishment. This sustained and strengthened Paul through the greatest storm of his life.

When the angel promised Paul that no one would lose their life, he also made clear that the ship would break apart. There are times that we experience significant loss, even though we are under the watchful care and sovereignty of God. Perhaps the job doesn't pan out, the marriage cannot be saved, and the contract or scholarship doesn't go through. The storms of life have a way of breaking things apart. The loss of the ship is not the end of the story, however. According to Acts 27:44, "all were brought safely to land." This reminds us that there is life after tragedy. Things may not go back to normal, but you will find that there is a new normal. I once heard someone say that when what you thought you needed breaks apart, the broken pieces are all you need.

Chapter 11

Drinking from the Cup of Suffering

On March 6, 1945, religious leaders throughout Romania were summoned to the parliament in the capital city of Bucharest. Among them was a couple named Richard and Sabina Wurmbrand. Communism was beginning to take hold of the country, and the Wurmbrands were leery of the religious freedoms that communism promised. Despite the guarantees or assurances that the Communist Party offered the Wurmbrands, they would not fall in line.

The propaganda event was given the name "The Congress of the Cults." Every religion and denomination in the country was asked to send a delegation to the parliament. Both religious and political leaders were paraded to the platform to praise communism. The event was broadcasted on live radio throughout the entire country. The longer Richard and Sabina sat through the speeches, the more a righteous anger rose within them. Finally, Sabina leaned over to Richard and said, "Stand up and wash this shame from the face of Christ." He responded, "If I do, you'll lose your husband." To which she said, "I don't want a coward for a husband."[43]

When Richard requested an opportunity to speak from the podium, the Communists could not have been happier. They supposed that if they had swayed the staunch Richard Wurmbrand, they had won a great victory for communism. By the time Richard reached the podium, the audience was flat. The four thousand leaders had sat for hours, listening to speech after speech after speech. Before this day had arrived, the Wurmbrands had already resolved in their heart that they would stand for Christ no matter the cost.

Richard boldly proclaimed Christ that day. He held nothing back, charging his fellow leaders to give their loyalty to Christ's kingdom, not an earthly government, especially that of Stalin's. So enraged were the Communist leaders that they demanded he leave the platform. Fearless and unflinching, Richard stood for Christ, as the applause grew louder and louder from his fellow ministers. Finally, the authorities had no choice but to take scissors and sever the cables to his microphone. Still, Wurmbrand continued to preach and the crowd continued to respond.

Three years later, Romania was firmly in the grip of communism. Richard and Sabina Wurmbrand would pay a high price for the stand they took. Richard was imprisoned for fourteen years, many of which he spent in solitary confinement. Sabina was imprisoned for three years, forcing her to leave her young son in the care of other believers. Wurmbrand masterfully tells his story in the classic book *Tortured for Christ*, published in 1967.[44] He revealed not only the severity of their suffering and persecution that was endured, but also that despite all their terrible experiences, it was Christ who was always their example. And through

His example, they learned how to suffer well. Fortunately, the international Christian community secured funds and negotiated Wurmbrand's release in 1964. Moving to the United States, Richard and Sabina founded the ministry Voice of the Martyrs, where they served the suffering and persecuted church until Sabina's death in 2000 and Richard's in 2001.

Why Jesus Came to Suffer

The pain and afflictions Jesus would endure were often referred to as a cup of suffering (Matt. 26:39; Mark 10:38; John 18:11). As Christ-followers, we drink from the same cup. Jesus made it clear that His followers would suffer in this life. If the world hated Christ, they would certainly hate us (John 15:18). The cup of suffering is a metaphor for the hardships we endure to fulfill God's eternal purposes. When we think of the sufferings of Jesus, we tend to only remember His physical sufferings at Calvary. In truth, His entire life was a series of sufferings.

Psalm 69 is a prophetic glimpse into Jesus's upbringing. It captures the sense of shame that permeated His life. According to verse 12, even the town drunks made up songs of mockery about His family. Imagine the rumors that might have circulated within their small community of Nazareth and even the surrounding villages. After all, His mother, Mary, had been pregnant and betrothed to Joseph even though they had not consummated their marriage. Yet this was the way God chose for His Son to come into the world. From His scandalous birth to His lack of education, to His family's poverty to His shameful death on a cross, Jesus's life and death was marked with shame and suffering.

Hear the words of 2 Corinthians 8:9—"For you know the grace of our Lord Jesus Christ, that though he was rich, yet for your sake he became poor, so that you by his poverty might become rich." God's ways are higher than our ways. One of the most unique and glorious titles for Christ is "Immanuel," which means "God with us" (Isa. 7:14). "And the Word became flesh and *dwelt* among us, and we have seen his glory, glory as of the only Son from the Father, full of grace and truth" (John 1:14, emphasis mine). The Greek word for "dwelt" is ἐσκήνωσεν (*eskēnōsen*), which comes from the root word σκηνόω (*skēnōō*), meaning "to pitch a tent" or "to tabernacle."

From the day of Christ's birth until His death, the implications of Him taking on a robe of flesh meant a life marked by suffering. Isaiah portrayed it vividly, saying, "Yet it was the will of the LORD to crush him; he has put him to grief" (Isa. 53:10a). This "crushing" speaks of Christ's physical pain. "Grief" speaks of His emotional pain. Christ endured suffering "to seek and to save the lost" (Luke 19:10).

Glory in the Common Places

In 2007, *The Washington Post* conducted a fascinating experiment.[45] They took the world-renowned violinist Joshua Bell into the subways of Washington, D.C. Dressed in a T-shirt and jeans, and wearing a baseball cap, Joshua played classical music for nearly forty-five minutes. The historic violin he played is worth an estimated four million dollars. People have paid large amounts of money to watch him play in concert venues, yet this time, in a most common place, only seven stopped to listen to the extraordinary music, and he collected $32.17. The results of the experiment were clear: We can take something extraordinary and uncommon, place it in a common setting, and most people will fail to pay attention.

The same happened in Bethlehem, when Christ was born. When the wise men traveled from the east (most likely Persia, which is modern-day Iran), their visit to Jerusalem aroused the suspicion of King Herod when they inquired about the birth of a new baby king. When they asked about the potential birthplace of Christ, King Herod knew enough to gather the priests and scribes to search the Scriptures (Matt. 2:4). They accurately pinpointed Micah 5:2—"But you, O Bethlehem Ephrathah, who are too little to be among the clans of Judah, from you shall come forth for me one who is to be ruler in Israel, whose coming forth is from of old, from ancient days." From here on, King Herod began to plot an evil plan against the Christ child.

King Herod's palace was only five miles from Bethlehem. It is unthinkable that these priests and scribes, who were so familiar with God's Word and understood and could explain Micah 5:2, were unwilling to worship or even visit Emmanuel with the wise men. So it is today. Many people love the Christmas season. They know the story, and even respect the story, yet they are unwilling to worship Jesus as Savior and Lord. The wise men were seeking Jesus for one purpose: "to worship him" (Matt. 2:2).

Bethlehem, also called the City of David, means "House of Bread." Because Christ was born in such a common place, very few acknowledged Him. The people of the day did not know the time of their visitation (Luke 19:44). They missed their Messiah. Let us be careful not to overlook, neglect, or miss Him in our own lives each day. Christ, who was born in Bethlehem, called "The House of Bread," had suffered throughout His life and died for our sins, but became "The Bread of Life" who will sustain and satisfy us through our suffering (John 6:35).

Christ Learned Obedience

When I first went blind, like most people, I asked the wrong questions: "Why is this happening to me?" "Did I do something to make God angry?" "Why would God allow this?" Today, it is amazing how I see God's goodness in what appeared to be a great loss. This positive perspective came because I did not get stuck in my questions.

Jesus healed many people who were blind. We read about one such man in John 9. When Jesus's disciples came across the man, they asked Jesus who had committed a sin to cause his blindness. Was it his own sin or that of his parents? Since he was born blind, they included his parents as a possibility. Jesus responded, saying that neither he nor his parents caused the blindness. Instead, the purpose of the blindness was so the works of God could be seen through him (John 9:3). God is not haphazard. He does not allow hardships by coincidence. Perhaps, like me, you feel stuck in your own questions. We would do well to realize God has purpose in everything that happens, for "all things work together for good to those who love God, to those who are the called according to His purpose" (Rom. 8:28 NKJV).

Ecclesiastes 7:13–14 reinforces the plans and purposes of God, even in our hardships: "Consider the work of God: who can make straight what he has made crooked? In the day of prosperity be joyful, and in the day of adversity consider: God has made the one as well as the other. . . ." The disciples' first reaction was to judge the blind man or his parents, and they arrived at the wrong conclusion. Jesus teaches us to consider the works of God. What if the disappointments you face or the delays you are experiencing are really the works of God being displayed through you?

At the time of this writing, my sons, Hudson and John Mark, are eight and six. They love playing baseball, basketball, and football. One of the most difficult parts of blindness for me is that I can't teach my sons how to catch or shoot a ball. Yet it is in these times that I hear the Lord ask me, "Is it worth My glory?" God is using this season of blindness in ways that I will not understand until I get to heaven. Even so, God is glorified in my suffering, and He is working His plans for my life. In those moments when the Lord asks me if it is worth it, I quietly and humbly whisper, "Yes."

The following verse about Jesus seems strange. It strikes me as out of place. As you read it, perhaps you will agree. "Although he was a son, he learned obedience through what he suffered" (Heb. 5:8). This verse is puzzling, because when I think of Christ needing to learn something, I think of Him being limited, but this is not the case. A. W. Pink gave understanding to this truth by arguing that if Christ had to grow in both wisdom and stature, then this verse alone shows that He grew in various ways (Luke 2:52).[46] To say that Christ learned obedience does not mean that He was disobedient in any way, or that He had to be forced to become obedient. Pink explains Christ learned obedience by submitting to the will of the Father.

This is crucial for us to understand the role of obedience in our own sufferings. When we ask questions like, "What have I done to deserve this?" or "How have I offended God or made Him angry?" the life and example of Christ teaches us that suffering does not come because we have sinned or angered God. Christ was sinless, but He suffered, and neither did the man born blind in John 9 commit sin. Can you see how our wrong questions lead us to wrong conclusions?

What was the experience that taught Christ obedience? Paul clarifies this when he writes: "who, though he was in the form of God, did not count equality with God a thing to be grasped, but emptied himself, by taking the form of a servant, being born in the likeness of men. And being found in human form, he humbled himself by becoming obedient to the point of death, even death on a cross" (Phil. 2:6–8).

Follow in His Footsteps

In 2024, I was invited to teach at a Bible conference in the Swiss Alps. My wife and I could not have been more excited about traveling to Switzerland. I recall a friend sharing with me years ago about his trip to Switzerland, describing how everywhere you go feels like a postcard. I knew I would be missing out on some beautiful scenery. When we got there, my friends kept talking about how blue the waters were and how breathtaking the mountains were. I began to feel like I had missed out on so much on the trip. One day, I traveled with the other pastors to Geneva. During the night session, one of the pastors shared this poem that I had never heard, written by Amy Carmichael in the late 1800s.

Scars

Hast thou no scar?
No hidden scar on foot, or side, or hand?
I hear thee sung as mighty in the land;
I hear them hail thy bright, ascendant star.
Hast thou no scar?

Hast thou no wound?
Yet I was wounded by the archers; spent,
Leaned Me against a tree to die; and rent
By ravening beasts that compassed Me, I swooned.
Hast thou no wound?

No wound? No scar?
Yet, as the Master shall the servant be,
And piercèd are the feet that follow Me.

But thine are whole; can he have followed far
Who hast no wound or scar?[47]

When I heard these words, I was comforted. How can I expect to follow Christ without walking in His footsteps? This means I will bear my own scars for His namesake, and so will you. Jesus reminds us of this when He said that no servant is greater than his master (John 15:20).

When writing his first epistle, Peter reminds the church: "For to this you have been called, because Christ also suffered for you, leaving you an example, so that you might follow in his steps" (1 Pet. 2:21). Peter does not say those who are suffering have upset God, or that they are outside of God's will. In fact, the opposite is true. He affirms that we suffer because we are "called" to it. The reason you can suffer well is because you are called to do it.

We follow in Jesus's footsteps because He is our ultimate example. When Peter calls Christ our example, he uses the Greek word ὑπογραμμὸς (*hypogrammos*). This term refers to a model or pattern, something that serves as an example to follow. It literally means "a writing underneath" or "a sketch," implying a template or an outline to imitate.

Picture children tracing letters of the alphabet. I love this imagery because of my stage of life. I had eyesight when my two girls learned how to read, but I have been blind while my boys are learning. They often trace their letters on my chest and arms, where I can help them figure out which way a "b" goes and how this differs from a "q." Our sufferings are the same. They may be elementary compared to what Christ endured, yet we learn from Him how to suffer well.

Peter instructs us to "follow in his steps" (v. 21). The Greek word for steps is ἴχνη (*ichne*). This term refers to footsteps or tracks, symbolizing the path or way that Christ walked and that believers are to follow. We know that the path of a Christian is a narrow way (Matt. 7:13–14). Furthermore, this path is marked with suffering, but when we choose to continue down this path, it pleases God: "When you do good and suffer for it you endure, this is a gracious thing in the sight of God" (1 Pet. 2:20).

The Fellowship of Suffering

When Paul wrote to the Christians of Corinth, his aim was to show them that they were part of a greater family of God rather than just an individual congregation. He wanted them to see that they were called into a deeper fellowship with one another and with Christ Himself. You and I are part of this same fellowship. It is the family of God.

We read: "To the church of God at Corinth, to those sanctified in Christ Jesus, called as saints, with all those in every place who call on the name of Jesus Christ our Lord—both their Lord and ours" (1 Cor. 1:2 CSB). When I read of "all those in every place," I think of the many believers I have met around the world. When preaching in the mountains of Colombia, I met a pastor slightly older than myself. He had been a revolutionary guerrilla until he encountered the grace of God. When preaching in his church, I couldn't believe the bond of faith I experienced with him. Neither of us could speak the other's language, yet the Holy Spirit was present in our fellowship. This created a bond of faith that transcended any language and culture.

Today, this same bond of faith should transcend differences and disagreements within the body of Christ. One of the most beautiful aspects of God's kingdom is that He does not expect us to be cookie-cutter Christ-followers. God's people are not like penguins. We do not all look alike or act alike. We can celebrate our differences and diversities as a global family of faith.

This is possible when Christ remains the center of our fellowship. Paul goes on to teach: "God is faithful; you were called by him into fellowship with his Son, Jesus Christ our Lord" (v. 9 CSB). The author of Hebrews describes this fellowship as a "heavenly calling" (Heb. 3:1). Our fellowship should involve more than just our local church. It should be bigger than one denomination. When we place our opinions and preferences above Christ, thus removing Him from the center of our fellowship, we are certain to get off course.

Paul takes the idea of fellowship with Christ deeper when writing to the Philippian believers: "My goal is to know him and the power of his resurrection and the fellowship of his sufferings, being conformed to his death" (Phil. 3:10 CSB). The Greek word for *fellowship* is *koinonia*. It can also be translated as "community," "union," "partnership," or "being yoked together." It describes the unity that comes from shared beliefs, convictions, and behaviors. When I picture fellowshipping with Christ, I think of my quiet time and devotion time, yet Paul calls us to more. He says fellowship with Christ is the sharing of His sufferings. It is in these sufferings that God can prepare us to be conformed into the image of Christ. Rather than despising our times of suffering, what if we saw them as opportunities to uniquely fellowship with Jesus?

Christ said to the church of Laodicea, "See! I stand at the door and knock. If anyone hears my voice and opens the door, I will come in to him and eat with him, and he with me" (Rev. 3:20 CSB). This is a beautiful picture of how Christ fellowships with His people. In today's world, we often schedule casual lunches, but this would have been more meaningful in the first century. Meals were a time of communing with those you cared for.

Have you ever wondered what it means for Christ to partake and dine with us? John Owen, a Puritan pastor from the 1600s, provided a treasure of an answer. He wrote that Christ partakes of the spiritual fruits produced in our lives by the Holy Spirit (Gal. 5:22–23).[48] The Holy Spirit uses suffering to help produce these fruits, and if we learn to suffer well, one of the greatest fruits it produces is joy.

Choosing Joy

C. S. Lewis's insightful book *The Problem of Pain* maintains that God is not haphazard. The suffering that God allows always comes with purpose. He writes: "God whispers to us in our pleasures, speaks in our conscience, but shouts in our pains: it is His megaphone to rouse a deaf world."[49]

Is God at this moment refining you? If so, receive the joy that only Christ can give. Jesus said, "I have told you these things so that my joy may be in you and your joy may be complete" (John 15:11 CSB). Note how Jesus said it is "My joy." We cannot be the source of our own joy. The source must be Christ. He is the vine, and we are the branches. I can be joyful in blindness, because my joy is sourced from Jesus.

Christ modeled His joy in the way He suffered on the cross: "who for the joy that was set before him endured the cross, despising the shame, and is seated at the right hand of the throne of God" (Heb. 12:2). What do you suppose was the joy set before Jesus? Jude answered that question: "Now to him who is able to protect you from stumbling and to make you stand in the presence of his glory, without blemish and with great joy" (Jude 1:24 CSB). Jesus suffered the cross to redeem sinners and present us as blameless before His Father. What a Savior!

All who desire to live a godly life will suffer (2 Tim. 3:12). You are not unspiritual because you suffer. God is not angry with you, and He is not tormenting you. God assures us that in this life we will face hardships and persecutions, but He also promises to give us a joy and a peace all the while. Submission is the first step to true discipleship, and Jesus taught us how to do this by taking up our cross daily to follow Him (Luke 9:23).

What does it mean to follow Christ by daily taking up our cross? It means that we die to ourselves, following in the footsteps of the great heroes of the faith before us like Dietrich Bonhoeffer and Adoniram and Ann Judson. Dietrich Bonhoeffer, who was executed by the Nazis on April 9, 1945, was one of Hitler's last victims. He wrote in *The Cost of Discipleship*: "When Christ calls a man, he bids him come and die."[50] I like the way the late evangelist Luis Palau explained, "When my will crosses His will, I choose His will."[51] We follow Christ daily by submitting to carrying the cross God chooses for us.

Adoniram Judson (1788–1850) was the first missionary sent out from the United States. He and his wife, Ann, left for Southeast Asia seven days after they were wed. Arriving in Burma in 1813, little did he know the price he would pay to sow the precious gospel seeds in the hardened soil of Burma. Because the Burmese would not touch the dead body of a foreigner, Adoniram buried his baby with his own hands. He would lose his wife, Ann, by 1826. He himself would be imprisoned, suffering tremendously for two years because of the Anglo-Burmese War.[52]

Despite Judson's suffering, he painstakingly translated the Bible into the Burmese language. It is the same translation the Burmese people use today. His son, Edward Judson, would later become a pastor in New York City. Years later, as he remembered his father, he wrote: "Success and suffering are vitally and organically linked. If you succeed without suffering, it is because someone suffered for you; if you suffer without succeeding, it is in order that someone else may succeed after you."[53] In 1813 there were no known Christians in Burma. By the time of Judson's death in 1850, after carrying his cross for forty years, he saw the fruit of his labor in 300,000 legally registered Burmese believers.

It is easy to see the purpose God had in someone like Adoniram Judson. It is not so easy to see God's purposes in our own pain. This is why we have the examples in both the

Scriptures and the lives of those who suffered well. The apostle Paul said he could rejoice in his personal sufferings because they were meant for the body of Christ. He expressed it so uniquely when he said, "I am filling up what is lacking in Christ's afflictions" (Col. 1:24).

John Piper sheds light on this passage when he notes that the world persecuted Christ, yet Christ is now in heaven and is the Head of His church.[54] Because we are the body of Christ, the persecution that the world once physically unleashed upon Christ now falls on His followers. The sufferings of Adoniram and Ann Judson resulted in the body of Christ being built up in Burma. Do not discount how the Lord is using your suffering. Do not overlook how you are being an example to family, neighbors, coworkers, and others who see Christ being formed in you, "the hope of glory" (v. 27).

A beautiful principle in Christianity is that we follow the pattern of Christ's life, death, and resurrection. Just as Jesus suffered in this life, so we are called to suffer. Just as He died upon the cross, we are to crucify our flesh. Just as Christ was raised from the dead, we will one day be raised. If we are faithful to endure, we have the promise to reign with Christ for all eternity (2 Tim. 2:11–12).

Consider this: The only suffering you will ever endure is in this life. God has promised an eternity of no suffering. This means whatever you are going through is an opportunity to uniquely glorify God in a way that you will not be able to when you get to heaven. Don't waste such an opportunity. Those who suffer with Him will reign with Him!

Chapter 12

Suffering with an Eternal Perspective

The kids went crazy when I walked into their village. Some were frightened, but most were excited, because I was the first white person they had ever seen. "*Mzungu! Mzungu!*" They ran around me, shouting. I told them to go tell everyone in their village to come hear the *mzungu*, meaning a person with white skin. The first time I preached the gospel in Africa was in the small villages of Malawi, the heart of Africa. I walked for miles through the African bush with pastors and church leaders, sharing Jesus from sunrise to sunset.

On one occasion, kids were sitting around me, feeling my hair and rubbing my arms. I asked the pastor why they kept rubbing me. A big smile came across his face as he explained, "They're trying to see if the white will rub off." I learned a valuable lesson preaching through the villages of Africa. When the sun goes down, your work is finished.

The common reality in the areas I visited was a lack of electricity and running water. After a few days, I realized very quickly how precious the time was before the sun set, as Jesus's words rang in my ears: "We must work the works of him who sent me while it is day; night is coming, when no one can work" (John 9:4). Could Peter have recalled these same words when Jesus encouraged people to glorify God with their sufferings in the time they had remaining (1 Pet. 4:2)?

Who Causes Suffering

The Gospels are filled with examples of Peter's mistakes. I once heard Peter described as someone who *ready, fires,* and then *aims*. When we come to the letters of 1 and 2 Peter, however, we find the apostle aging. Peter had once walked with Christ and helped established the early church, but was now writing with wisdom from the Holy Spirit to suffering Christians. Consider sitting down and reading 1 Peter in its entirety (only five chapters). When you do, read it through the lens of suffering, for indeed it is the theme of the epistle.

If we hope to suffer well in this life, it will require an eternal perspective. We are called to be people who handle times of trouble by seeing life as a vapor (James 4:14). Because life and its sufferings are so short, our focus will fall on eternity. This is how Paul viewed hardships: "For this light momentary affliction is preparing for us an eternal weight of glory beyond all comparison" (2 Cor. 4:17). We can have the same attitude through our difficult days.

We all go through suffering. Since the point of this book is to learn how to suffer well, this chapter will explore this with respect to 1 Peter 4:19. Peter reveals how suffering can help us trust in God's will and move forward in faith.

People often ask me whether I think God or Satan caused my blindness. My answer surprises most. I believe both God and Satan are at work. When you study the life of Job, it is clear that God had an agenda and so did Satan. It is the same in our lives. God wants us to grow; Satan wants us to fail. The testing of our faith will cause one or the other.

When I consider that God and Satan desire different outcomes from my blindness, my mind goes to James 4:6–7: "But he gives more grace. Therefore, it says, 'God opposes the proud but gives grace to the humble.' Submit yourselves therefore to God. Resist the devil, and he will flee from you." Verse 7 in particular helps me reconcile my faith and feelings. We are commanded to submit to God and to resist the devil. Do you see how both are at work at the same time? Thus, we are to respond to both at the same time, submitting to one and resisting the other. Verse 6 is the key to submitting to God through difficult situations, with James saying, "God opposes the proud but gives grace to the humble."

Consider the humility required to walk roads marked with suffering. Often, the reason people are hurt and offended by God is because they have overlooked the necessity of humility. Notice the first phrase of James 4:6—He gives "more grace." God has all the grace we need, yet often we lack humility. As we learn to humble ourselves, we find more grace that enables us to submit under God's mighty hand and to fiercely resist the devil.

Consider the outcome of a person who submits to God and resists the devil. James says Satan will flee (v. 7). Can you remember times when it felt like you were bombarded by the Enemy?

He launched his fiery arrows and each one of them landed. How many of us unknowingly cower to the Enemy? We so easily give up ground Christ has already won. The reality is that we can resist Satan, and we know he will flee. We need not entertain Satan's plots, tricks, or deceits. The biblical promise stands that if we resist him, he must flee.

Comfortable Christianity

What comes to mind when you think of the 1950s? Although I was not yet born, I am a great admirer of that decade. After World War II, America emerged as the leading superpower of the world. The fifties boasted its music, rock stars, fast cars, and a host of electronics and new conveniences for daily life. The American Dream was for the taking. The 1950s saw the establishment of a National Day of Prayer, led by the fiery, young evangelist, Billy Graham. "In God We Trust" was printed on our money. Christianity was rooted in the institutions of American life.

However, a subtle change began to make its way into the church. A change that is not so subtle today. It is complacency—a mindset of comfortable Christianity, an attitude that if God loves me, He wants me to be happy above all else. The Christians of the early New Testament era would have completely rejected this way of thinking. Later, we will see that Peter speaks against this mindset in 1 Peter 4.

When thinking about the 1950s, I recall the story of Jim and Elisabeth Elliot. Elisabeth Elliot, born in 1926, was a hero of the faith. She grew up in a godly home and aspired to be a missionary. While attending Wheaton College, she fell in love with a young man from the West Coast named Jim Elliot. Although both sensed a call to overseas mission work, it would take several long and patient years before they would become husband and wife. They were married in 1953 and soon settled in Ecuador, with the aim of winning unreached tribes to Christ.

Soon after, a baby girl was born to the Elliots. Jim tried to make life in the mission field as comfortable as he could for his young family. He built their home and was such a skilled carpenter that they even enjoyed indoor plumbing and indoor showers. Quite a luxury in the jungles of South America.

Jim is famous for saying, "He is no fool who gives what he cannot keep to gain what he will never lose."[55] These words proved true on January 8, 1956. Jim and his four other companions—Nate Saint, Ed McCully, Peter Fleming, and Roger Youderian—were killed by members of the Huaorani Warriors. Their sacrifice forever changed the landscape of missions. Remarkably, Elisabeth and the other widows stayed in Ecuador to continue the work of their fallen husbands. Elisabeth was left by herself to raise their ten-month-old daughter, Valerie. Well-meaning friends and family could not comprehend her willingness to withstand the pressures of missionary life in the jungle as a new mother and widow. Despite their urging for her to return home, Elisabeth was resolute in her decision to stay.

Firm in her faith, Elisabeth lived and ministered among the very tribe who killed her husband. God had not only called Jim, but also Elisabeth, to a life of mission work. Although Jim was no longer there, the Lord was. While their experiences at times seemed unbearable, Elisabeth trusted in God's faithfulness to sustain, protect, and provide for her and her daughter.

Elisabeth wrote: "God teaches us our deepest lessons in our deepest sufferings."[56] Although she went to be with the Lord in 2015, we can still draw insight from her experiences. In her book *Suffering Is Never for Nothing*,[57] she explains how all of us suffer to one degree or another. Suffering can be as simple as wanting something you cannot have. It's when you pray for restoration, but the divorce goes through. It's when you believe for the job, but the phone call never comes.

Suffering can also be when you have something you don't want, such as blindness in my case. The point is that each of us suffers. Yet, Elisabeth says most of us ask the wrong question when we suffer. We ask, "God, what can be done about this?" She says the right question should be, "God, what can be done with this?"

As we will see from 1 Peter, Scripture wants to give us the right perspective, which, in turn, gives the right attitude.

A Different Way of Thinking

My mom was not merely a Sunday-morning Christian. She was an "every time the doors are open" type of churchgoer. In some ways, I feel like I grew up *at* church. Yet in all those years, I can never recall one single sermon preached from 1 Peter 4:1, that those who suffer in the flesh cease from sinning. We don't often hear those kinds of sermons in today's pulpits. Yet it is word-for-word what the Scriptures say.

Peter writes: "Since therefore Christ suffered in the flesh, arm yourselves with the same way of thinking, for whoever has suffered in the flesh has ceased from sin" (1 Pet. 4:1). There isn't but one way to lay hold of the truth of this statement, and that is to adjust our thinking to that of the Scriptures. This is precisely what Peter meant when he wrote: "arm yourselves with [this] same way of thinking." Since Peter wrote to an audience of suffering Christians, imagine the courage his writings brought to their hearts when they read: "For to this you have been called, because Christ also suffered for you, leaving you an example, so that you might follow in his steps" (2:21).

Peter uses a military term *hoplizo*, translated as "arm" (1 Pet. 4:1). We who suffer are to take up weapons and engage in a spiritual battle. How can we suffer well for Christ if we are carnal in our minds and wrapped up in worldly pursuits? The call is crystal clear: We should adjust our minds and our attitudes. The NIV renders it: "arm yourselves also with the same attitude." This is why Paul told Timothy, "Share in suffering as a good soldier of Christ Jesus. No soldier gets entangled in civilian pursuits, since his aim is to please the one who enlisted him" (2 Tim. 2:3–4). Have you considered how your attitude is a weapon in the hands of God? No wonder Satan wants to sour it.

When we suffer with the right attitude, we cease from sinning. This does not mean that we will be sinless in this life. However, we are to be sinning less and less if we are taking our spiritual walk seriously. Unfortunately, today's average

Christian's goal is to simply go to heaven. Biblically, heaven is not the goal of salvation. An eternity in heaven is not a goal; it is a fact. This would be like children setting a goal to be part of their family. The reality is, they were born into their family. When we are born again, we become part of the family of God, giving us assurance of salvation.

Rather, the goal of salvation ought to be overcoming sin. John Owen, the great Puritan pastor of the 1600s, said, "Be killing sin or sin will be killing you."[58] We should be ruthless in our fight against sin. And one of the greatest ways God purifies the life of a believer is through suffering. We should not despise it.

According to 1 Peter 4:1, if I adjust my thinking to fighting sin, then according to verse 2, I am going to be able to reject sin and center my life in the will of God: "so as to live for the rest of the time in the flesh no longer for human passions but for the will of God" (v. 2). In his book *When the Game Is Over, It All Goes Back in the Box,* John Ortberg wisely observes how we all pack as much as we can into the days we are given.[59] We fill the squares of our calendars with as many meetings, appointments, and errands as possible. All the while, we are all heading toward eternity. The question is whether we are living for eternity. They said of Jonathan Edwards that he had "eternity stamped on his eye."[60] This is because he viewed every day of his life in light of eternity. When you and I gain such a perspective, we will ensure we are in the will of God.

No Bad Luck in the Kingdom of God

One day, as my eyesight was deteriorating, I went to see my primary care physician. I could barely see him out of my right eye as he examined my left. He asked me what the eye doctors at Duke University had told me. When I told him how they said nothing could be done, he responded: "Chad, you either have really bad DNA or you have really bad luck." The Bible gives me assurance that this isn't the case, since 1 Peter 4:19 indicates that at times we suffer "according to God's will."

For years a portrait of the missionary James Hudson Taylor has hung in my office. His writings have taught that the will of God is really more of a matter for God to consider than for us, because if God leads us into a place of comfort and luxury, we need His grace. Should God choose to lead us into a place of difficulty and hardship, we still need His grace. So then, either way, we live by the grace of God.

A few years into my blindness, I was riding in the car with my family when my oldest daughter, Piper, who was around ten years old at the time, asked, "Dad, what would you give if God gave you back your eyesight?" Immediately, the words of Hudson Taylor came to my mind. I explained to my children how that was a matter more so for God to consider than for me. Why? In short, I have learned how to be content with eyesight, and I have learned how to be greatly content without it. If I have eyesight, it is by the grace of God, and if I don't, I still live by that same grace.

Think It Not Strange

Many have walked before us that have faced great suffering, and Jesus promised that it would come. Yet, they've walked it with faith. It's those like the Elliots and the Judsons and Hudson Taylor and Dietrich Bonhoeffer that remind us when we face struggle that we can continue pressing on. Similarly, Peter wrote at a time when suffering in the early church was not only bad, but getting worse throughout the Roman Empire. Through the inspiration of the Holy Spirit, his epistle not only carried them through difficult days, but inspired every generation of the church since.

Listen for the tenderness of his tone as he writes: "Beloved, do not be surprised at the fiery trial when it comes upon you to test you, as though something strange were happening to you" (1 Pet. 4:12). Note how he calls them "beloved." This means to be accepted by God; it is to be dearly loved by Him. Your ability to handle troubling times will often come down to how you think God feels about you. If you believe God is angry at you or somehow punishing you, it is going to be difficult to suffer well.

Pastor and author Erwin Lutzer observes that, for many people, disaster causes them to run from God, but for others, it causes us to run into His arms.[61] This is the perspective Scripture wants you to have. Painful experiences should draw you toward God, not away from Him.

Many people have asked me if I am angry at God for allowing me to go blind, especially in my late thirties. How can I be when Scripture teaches me how to feel about misfortune? If I know I am loved by God, then I can continue in this path of biblical thinking that I should not be surprised when fiery trials come into my life. Have you thought about the purpose God has in the fire that touches your life? Maybe God's intention is to spark new growth.

According to the National Forest Foundation, there is a phenomenon that happens after a forest fire. God has built into certain trees and shrubs seeds that can only be unlocked through fire. They are known as pyrophytes. These seeds can lie dormant for years, because they are covered by a hard coating. But when lightning strikes or some other cause sets fire to a forest, the heat burns the resin off the seeds, allowing them to sprout and regrow the forest.[62]

Perhaps you are looking around your life today and everything appears devastated and destroyed. I know the feeling of waking up to a new day, but everything seems charred and only ashes remain. Could it be that God has purpose to this fire? Could it be that God is doing more than it appears?

Peter explains how we should feel when we face fiery trials. We should not feel as though God is punishing or picking on us. Instead, we should remember that we belong to the Lord and He has purpose in the fire. When you come to a place where fiery testing does not seem strange (v. 12), you will be more apt to rejoice in these tests: "But rejoice insofar as you share Christ's sufferings, that you may also rejoice and be glad when his glory is revealed" (v. 13). Can you see the clear logic of these verses? Most people cannot rejoice and give glory to God in their sufferings because they think something strange is happening to them.

Peter reinforces the idea of rejoicing in suffering when he writes: "In this you rejoice, though now for a little while, if necessary, you have been grieved by various trials" (1:6). That small phrase "if necessary" is striking to me. Have you ever asked why trials are necessary? It is because our suffering is never meaningless. It comes into our life with great design, meaning, and purpose. God does not waste anything, especially pain.

Peter says that we should rejoice in these hardships. Are you kidding me? Peter, are you saying I should rejoice in blindness? Is it possible to rejoice in life's hurt and loss? The Scriptures shout a resounding, "*Yes!*" This is exactly what God intends, because God never allows pain without great purpose behind it. When I look beyond my present trial to the plans and purposes of God, I rejoice, even when the Enemy tries to cause me to only see those situations that are outside of my control. However, God wants me to look at Him who is my hope and the security of my soul.

Dr. Martyn Lloyd-Jones joins the ranks of those worthy of emulation. He was born in 1899 and was pastor of the famous Westminster Chapel in London for twenty-five years. His preaching and writing are strong and sturdy works of faith. He lived until 1981, and toward the end of his life, his biographer, Iain H. Murray, daily spent time with him. Lloyd-Jones could no longer preach or travel because his body was racked with pain from cancer, but this did not stop him from editing his sermons for publication.

Every day, Pastor Lloyd-Jones got up from his sick bed, changed from his pajamas into a three-piece suit, and sat in an armchair next to his bed, where he edited his sermons for publication. He could only work a few hours until exhaustion would force him to change back into his pajamas and return to bed. Murray, watching the pastor's daily routine, asked him how it felt to go from being a world-famous in-demand preacher to seemingly feeling as though God had put him on a shelf. Lloyd-Jones responded: "I rejoice that my name is written in the Lamb's Book of Life."[63]

Are you able to rejoice in the midst of trials? Do you remember that they are but temporary, but the hope we have as those whose names are written in the Lamb's Book of Life is eternal? How thankful I am that trials do not last. Whatever difficulty you are facing, rest assured that it is only for an appointed season. When teaching the parable of the persistent widow in Luke 18, Jesus reminded us that when we need God to rescue us, He will come to our aid "quickly" (v. 8 NIV). It is in seasons of affliction that God can seem the slowest in answering prayer. Has your spiritual life ever felt like a drought and God seemed distant? Each of us can be vulnerable to these feelings, but the reality is God is with us. May I remind you of Psalm 145:18? "The LORD is near to all who call on him, to all who call on him in truth."

For me, the most difficult part of 1 Peter 1:6 is the phrase "if necessary." Peter was reminding these suffering saints that their afflictions are necessary to their spiritual growth. In the next verse, he states why their sufferings were unavoidable: "so that the tested genuineness of your faith—more precious than gold that perishes though it is tested by fire—may be found to result in praise and glory and honor at the revelation of Jesus Christ" (v. 7). Can you see that God is working through your afflictions?

It is easy to blame the Lord for our troubles because we know how easy it would be for Him to change them, let alone prevent them. But the wise Christian will pause and consider why these difficulties are necessary for our growth. The purpose of our suffering is to bring forth the genuineness of our faith.

Trusting in Suffering

As I continue on this path of blindness, I have made one great resolve. It is to not stop. I refuse to stop seeking God and His will for my life. I base this decision on these words: "Therefore let those who suffer according to God's will entrust their souls to a faithful Creator while doing good" (4:19). Resolved in my faith, I continue to move forward with no plans to stop, regardless of my sufferings. However, this decision is not rooted in emotions or even in a positive attitude. It is rooted in the confidence that I can entrust my soul to my Creator because He alone is faithful.

The word *entrust* is a financial term. It is the idea of taking a sum of money to the bank and making a deposit. Anyone who invests a significant amount of money will ensure that their banking institution is FDIC insured. It would be ludicrous to put your money in an unprotected bank. If you can trust the banking institution where you deposit money, how much more can you trust God? We can trust God in our suffering because Jesus did. According to 1 Peter 2:23, Christ "entrusted" Himself to the Father. He deposited His faith into the hands of God. Furthermore, Christ is our "example" in suffering (v. 21).

Peter's conclusion is that if we can trust God with something as valuable, precious, and eternal as our soul, then surely we can trust Him with our everyday lives. Think about it. If I can trust God for eternity, then why could I not trust Him for today?

Why do you suppose Peter refers to God as a "faithful Creator" (4:19)? When I get to heaven, I want to ask Peter if his mind went to Psalm 121:1–2: "I lift up my eyes to the hills. From where does my help come? My help comes from the LORD, who made heaven and earth." As the Creator, God controls all things. When blindness slammed into my life, my faithful Creator was not shocked nor surprised.

If I can entrust my soul to my Creator, then I can entrust my present circumstances to Him. I can entrust my eyes. I can entrust blindness. I can entrust disappointments. I can entrust hurts and wounds. I can give it all to the faithful Creator and so can you. Don't forget that because you are in the will of God, you shouldn't get angry. Humble yourself. Submit yourself. Entrust your soul to a faithful Creator. Second Timothy 2:13 assures us that when we are faithless, God remains faithful.

It is not abnormal to experience times of weakness, frustration, and confusion. In these times of hurt, you might have blamed God, speaking or even shouting regrettable words to Him. Let me assure you that God is not angry at you. In 2 Timothy 2:13, we see the heart of God at work. He loves you and you belong to Him. You're His child. He's not going to forsake you, and He's not going to abandon you. No matter what you have said, you are God's beloved.

It is far better to have hard conversations with God than to ignore Him altogether. Terry Whitson, my spiritual mentor, taught me that when there are times I do not feel like praying, to be honest. Tell God how you feel, what is frustrating you, why you are disappointed or let down. Then Terry smiled and said, "Do you know what you just did?" You just prayed and had a conversation with God.

Don't Stop in Your Sufferings

Shortly after my failed surgeries I had difficulty preaching due to debilitating pain. For weeks I spoke with a chair behind me to support me in my dizziness. Each weekend, the worship team was prepared to continue singing if I could not speak, and other staff members were prepared to speak in my place because it was so touch-and-go.

My turning point came on one particular Sunday. During the music, I rushed out the side of the building, sick with nausea and feeling disoriented. Here I am the lead pastor, losing his breakfast in a side parking lot, while the congregation is singing worship to God. That morning, I had a choice if I was going to go forward and preach or if I was going to back down and let Satan win.

In that moment, I straightened myself up and I said audibly, "Devil, if I have to physically crawl to my podium to preach, I will crawl. I will not stop for anything. You might as well leave me alone, because I will not quit!"

We must never forget that Satan wants to rob our faith! He wants to discourage us from praying. He wants you to isolate yourself, become a spiritual recluse, and live in shame and defeat. As Christians, how do we resist this? God's Word tells us that our lives are in the center of God's will. Yes, you are suffering, but you are suffering according to God's will. That makes all the difference. As you entrust your soul to a faithful Creator, don't stop in your suffering, but continue doing good. Don't quit. Don't back down. Keep going forward, in Jesus's name. If you can trust God for eternal salvation, then you can trust Him for your present situation. If you can trust Him for eternity, then you can trust Him for today, and you can trust Him for tomorrow. Just keep going.

Notes

1. Helen Lemmel, "Turn Your Eyes Upon Jesus," *The Hymnal of the Church of the Nazarene*, ed. Melvin H. McKinney (Nazarene Publishing House, 1998).

2. J. R. Miller, "You Will Not Mind the Roughness," in L. B. Cowman, *Streams in the Desert: 366 Daily Devotional Readings* (Zondervan, 2004), 463.

3. Miller, "You Will Not Mind the Roughness," 463.

4. J. C. Ryle, *Practical Religion* (William Hunt and Company, 1878), 219.

5. Alan Redpath, *Victorious Christian Living* (Moody Publishers, 1977).

6. Kevin Landis, *The Cowboy Steward* (iUniverse, 2006), 62.

7. Adrian Rogers, *The Power of His Presence* (Crossway, 1995), 45.

8. Epicurus, *The Epicurus Reader: Selected Writings and Testimonia*, transl. Brad Inwood and L. P. Gerson (Hackett Publishing, 1994), 30.

9. Chuck Missler, *Job: An Expositional Commentary* (Koinonia House, 2003), audiobook.

10. John Piper, *Providence* (Crossway, 2021), 300.

11. Thomas Boston, *The Crook in the Lot: The Sovereignty and Wisdom of God Displayed in the Afflictions of Men* (1737), 100.

12. James M. Gray, "The Refiner's Fire," in L. B. Cowman, *Streams in the Desert* (Zondervan, 1925), 50.

13. A. W. Tozer, *The Root of Righteousness* (Christian Publications, Inc., 1955), 13.

14. George Sweeting, *Psalms of the Heart* (Moody Press, 1982), 65.

15. This was often said by Pastor Johnny Gibson, Way of Life Baptist Church, Bloomingdale, Tennessee.

16. Amy Carmichael, *If* (Society for Promoting Christian Knowledge, 1938), 20.

17. Les Brown, *Live Your Dreams* (William Morrow and Company, 1992), 120.

18. Arthur T. Pierson, *George Müller of Bristol* (Fleming H. Revell Company, 1899), 200.

19. "The Martyrdom of Polycarp," ch. 11, in *The Apostolic Fathers: Greek Texts and English Translations*, 3rd ed., trans. Michael W. Holmes (Baker Academic, 2007), 235.

20. John N. Oswalt, *The Book of Isaiah, Chapters 40–66* (Eerdmans, 1998), 120.

21. Leonard Ravenhill, *Why Revival Tarries* (Bethany Fellowship, 1959), 80.

22. John MacArthur, *The Power of Integrity* (Crossway, 1997), 90.

23. Warren W. Wiersbe, *The Bumps Are What You Climb On* (Baker Books, 1980), 75.

24. John Sargent, *The Life and Letters of Henry Martyn* (Seeley and Burnside, 1819), 150.

25. Corrie Ten Boom, with John and Elizabeth Sherrill, *The Hiding Place* (Chosen Books, 1971), 217.

26. MacArthur, *The Power of Integrity*, 95.

27. "The Martyrdom of Polycarp, ch. 14, in *The Apostolic Fathers: Greek Texts and English Translations*, 3rd ed., trans. Michael W. Holmes (Baker Academic, 2007), 237.

28. "Oh, the Blood of Jesus," public domain.

29. Lysa Terkeurst, *It's Not Supposed to Be This Way* (Thomas Nelson, 2018), 50.

30. Jennifer Rothschild, *Lessons I Learned in the Dark* (Multnomah, 2002), 30.

31. Andrew Murray, *With Christ in the School of Prayer* (Merchant Books, 2013). (Original work published in 1890.)

32. A. W. Pink, *The Life of Elijah* (Bible Truth Depot, 1956), 15.

33. Warren W. Wiersbe, *Be Faithful* (Victor Books, 1984), 60.

34. John Piper, *The Hidden Smile of God* (Crossway, 2001), 45.

35. John Phillips, *Exploring Acts* (Kregel Publications, 1986), 70.

36. Bryan Walsh, "Global Warming: The Culprit?" *Time*, 166 (14), October 3, 2005, 44–53.

37. Romans 16:20; 1 Corinthians 16:23; 2 Corinthians 13:14; Galatians 6:18; Ephesians 6:24; Philippians 4:23; Colossians 4:18; 1 Thessalonians 5:28; and 2 Thessalonians 3:18.

38. Charles Spurgeon, "Strength in Weakness," *Metropolitan Tabernacle Pulpit Sermons,* Vol. 37, (Passmore & Alabaster 1891), 37:331.

39. John Newton, *The Life of John Newton* (Banner of Truth Trust, 2007), 25.

40. J. D. Cowan, *Newton: The Man Who Found Grace* (Christian Focus Publications, 2002), 243.

41. J. Bull, *John Newton of Olney and St. Mary Woolnoth: An Autobiography and Memoir* (The Religious Tract Society, 1868), 378.

42. John Newton, "Amazing Grace," 1772.

43. Sabina Wurmbrand, *The Pastor's Wife* (Fleming H. Revell, 1970), 36.

44. Richard Wurmbrand, *Tortured for Christ* (Hodder & Stoughton, 1967), 40.

45. Gene Weingarten, "Pearls Before Breakfast," *The Washington Post*, April 8, 2007, 10.

46. A. W. Pink, *The Sovereignty of God* (Baker Books, 1930), 85.

47. Amy Carmichael, *Toward Jerusalem* (Society for Promoting Christian Knowledge, 1936), 12.

48. John Owen, *The Mortification of Sin* (Christian Heritage, 1656), 35.

49. C. S. Lewis, *The Problem of Pain* (HarperOne, 1996), 91.

50. Dietrich Bonhoeffer, *The Cost of Discipleship* (SCM Press, 1948), 20.

51. Luis Palau, and S. Ford, *A Friendly Dialogue with God* (Multnomah Publishers, 2001), 45.

52. Courtney Anderson, *To the Golden Shore: The Life of Adoniram Judson* (Little, Brown and Company, 1956), 100.

53. Edward Judson, *The Life of Adoniram Judson* (American Baptist Publication Society, 1883), 50.

54. John Piper, *Desiring God* (Multnomah, 1986), 75.

55. Elisabeth Elliot, *Shadow of the Almighty: The Life and Testament of Jim Elliot* (Harper & Brothers, 1958), 65.

56. Elisabeth Elliot, *A Path Through Suffering* (Servant Publications, 1990), 13.

57. Elisabeth Elliot, *Suffering Is Never for Nothing* (B&H Publishing Group, 2019).

58. John Owen, *The Mortification of Sin* (Christian Heritage, 1656), 25.

59. John Ortberg, *When the Game Is Over, It All Goes Back in the Box* (Zondervan, 2007), 80.

60. George M. Marsden, *Jonathan Edwards: A Life* (Yale University Press, 2003), 45.

61. Erwin Lutzer, *When a Nation Forgets God* (Moody Publishers, 2010), 55.

62. National Forest Foundation, *Fire Ecology and Management* (National Forest Foundation Press, 2020), 15.

63. Iain H. Murray, *David Martyn Lloyd-Jones: The Fight of Faith, 1939–1981* (Banner of Truth Trust, 1990), 736.